Working with Political Science Research Methods

Fourth Edition

SAGE was founded in 1965 by Sara Miller McCune to support
the dissemination of usable knowledge by publishing innovative
and high-quality research and teaching content. Today, we
publish more than 850 journals, including those of more than
300 learned societies, more than 800 new books per year, and
a growing range of library products including archives, data,
case studies, reports, and video. SAGE remains majority-owned
by our founder, and after Sara's lifetime will become owned by
a charitable trust that secures our continued independence.

Los Angeles | London | New Delhi | Singapore | Washington DC

Working with Political Science Research Methods

Problems and Exercises

Fourth Edition

Jason D. Mycoff
University of Delaware

Los Angeles | London | New Delhi
Singapore | Washington DC

Los Angeles | London | New Delhi
Singapore | Washington DC

FOR INFORMATION:

CQ Press
An Imprint of SAGE Publications, Inc.
2455 Teller Road
Thousand Oaks, California 91320
E-mail: order@sagepub.com

SAGE Publications Ltd.
1 Oliver's Yard
55 City Road
London EC1Y 1SP
United Kingdom

SAGE Publications India Pvt. Ltd.
B 1/I 1 Mohan Cooperative Industrial Area
Mathura Road, New Delhi 110 044
India

SAGE Publications Asia-Pacific Pte. Ltd.
3 Church Street
#10-04 Samsung Hub
Singapore 049483

Acquisitions Editor: Sarah Calabi
Senior Development Editor: Nancy Matuszak
Editorial Assistant: Raquel Christie
Production Editor: Kelly DeRosa
Copy Editor: Shannon Kelly
Typesetter: C&M Digitals (P) Ltd.
Proofreader: Jennifer Grubba
Cover Designer: Gail Buschman
Marketing Manager: Amy Whitaker

Printed in the United States of America

Library of Congress Cataloging-in-Publication Data

ISBN 978-1-5063-0671-1

Library of Congress Control Number: 2015947379

This book is printed on acid-free paper.

17 18 19 10 9 8 7 6 5 4 3 2

Contents

CQ Press, an imprint of SAGE, is the leading publisher of books, periodicals, and electronic products on American government and international affairs. CQ Press consistently ranks among the top commercial publishers in terms of quality, as evidenced by the numerous awards its products have won over the years. CQ Press owes its existence to Nelson Poynter, former publisher of the *St. Petersburg Times,* and his wife Henrietta, with whom he founded *Congressional Quarterly* in 1945. Poynter established CQ with the mission of promoting democracy through education and in 1975 founded the Modern Media Institute, renamed The Poynter Institute for Media Studies after his death. The Poynter Institute (*www.poynter.org*) is a nonprofit organization dedicated to training journalists and media leaders.

In 2008, CQ Press was acquired by SAGE, a leading international publisher of journals, books, and electronic media for academic, educational, and professional markets. Since 1965, SAGE has helped inform and educate a global community of scholars, practitioners, researchers, and students spanning a wide range of subject areas, including business, humanities, social sciences, and science, technology, and medicine. A privately owned corporation, SAGE has offices in Los Angeles, London, New Delhi, and Singapore, in addition to the Washington DC office of CQ Press.

About the Author

Jason D. Mycoff is associate professor of political science and international relations at the University of Delaware. His research is on American political institutions, in particular the U.S. Congress, congressional committees, and parties.

CHAPTER 1

Introduction

Practice Makes Perfect

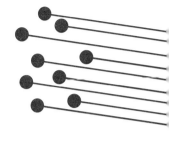

While most political science courses deal with government, issues, and politics, research methods is an important component of political science that helps students better understand course work and has practical applications. Most political arguments raise claims of fact, as when someone says, "We *should* repeal the Obama health plan because it will *increase* health spending." The first part of the statement takes a normative position (something ought to be done), whereas the second makes a factual claim; it states that one thing leads to another, whether or not anyone wants this to be the case. The goal of our textbook, *Political Science Research Methods,* is to show you how those two types of assertions can be separated and how the latter can be demonstrated empirically. The goal of this workbook is to help you apply those cognitive skills.

At first sight, achieving these objectives may seem easy. And it is! But it also requires a degree of thought and care. Moreover, the best way to acquire the necessary skills is to practice actively and then practice some more. After all, no sports team would prepare for a game simply by reading a scouting report. But I believe if you make an honest effort, the process of verification can be fascinating as well as informative.

Most of the exercises in this workbook ask you to think before writing. The thought process is typically straightforward and certainly does not require a strong mathematical aptitude. A thorough reading of the text, attention to class notes, and a dose of common sense should be adequate.

Note also that many questions call for judgment and explanation; they do not necessarily have one "correct" answer. Unless a question is based on a straightforward calculation or reading of a table, you will often be asked to think about a possible solution and to defend your choice.

The chapters in this workbook follow the chapters in the main text. That is, there are exercises for each chapter except the first and last. It is important to read the chapter in the text *before* starting to do an assignment. Many questions require you to integrate a chapter's different elements. Hence, you cannot just try to look up something without grasping the subject matter as a whole.

An orderly, step-by-step approach is the best way to work through the exercises in this workbook; it will help you avoid errors and make the important concepts relayed in the text clearer. If you are asked to make any calculations, you should do them neatly on a separate piece of paper that you can, with instructor approval, turn in along with your answers. Here's a tip: your intermediate calculations or scrap work should be written in such a way that someone can reconstruct your thought processes. Figure 1–1 provides a simple example. It shows that the respondent first clarified the requested information and then performed the computation on a separate sheet of paper.

Figure 1–2 gives an example of someone using the workbook itself as a scratch pad and the ensuing confusion that often comes from sloppy writing and thinking. Note that some of the numbers were copied incorrectly and that the arithmetical operations are out of order. (The correct answer, by the way, is $28,650, not $24,150.)

All the data you need to do the exercises in this workbook are included in the workbook or textbook or can be downloaded from the student Web site at http://edge.sagepub.com/johnson8e. When you are looking for a specific data set on the student Web site, simply click on the appropriate folder on the site. For instance, if you are looking for anes2004.dat, anes2004.por, or anescodebook.txt, open the folder called "ANES Data" and you will find each of those files. Once you learn how to use a program it is easy to explore a variety of hypotheses and problems. Besides being intrinsically interesting, knowledge of research methods provides skills that will help you in other courses and in many professions.

Have fun!

FIGURE 1-1

Be Organized and Neat

Party	Freq.
Democrat..................	200
Republican...............	150
Independent.............	100
None........................	50
Total.....................	500

[Separate sheet of paper]

Percent = Number over total times 100.

200 Dems/500 = 2/5 = .4

$.4 \times 100 = 40\%$

Refer to the table above.
What percentage of the sample are Democrats?   40%

FIGURE 1-2

Sloppiness Leads to Errors

What is the mean, or average, per capita income of the following six countries?   24,150

	144,900	
Luxembourg	$32,700	= 24,150
United States	31,500	———
Bermuda	30,000	5̶ 6
Switzerland	26,400	3̶2̶,̶5̶0̶0̶ 32,700
Singapore	26,300	31,500
Hong Kong	25,000	3,000
		26,400
		26,300
		2̶5̶,̶5̶0̶0̶ 2̶5̶,̶8̶0̶0̶ 25,000
		———
		1̶,414,900

CHAPTER 2

The Empirical Approach to Political Science

In chapter 2 of the textbook, we describe the scientific method and argue that it underlies empirical political science research. We note that empiricism is not the only method of obtaining knowledge—there are others that lots of people fervently adhere to—and a case can be made against trying to study politics scientifically. (There are even disagreements about the definition and nature of the scientific method.) Nevertheless, this way of acquiring knowledge is so common that many social scientists take it for granted, as do many average citizens. The problem is that scientific claims are sometimes difficult to distinguish from other kinds of statements. Nor is it always clear whether and how empirical analysis can be applied to propositions stated in theoretical and practical terms. The following questions, problems, and assignments therefore offer opportunities for you to think about the application of the empirical approach. Note that not all of the questions have one "right" answer. Many, in fact, require a lot of careful thought. And it is often necessary to redefine or clarify words or phrases, to look for hidden assumptions, and to consider whether or not statements can be "translated" into scientific terms.

Exercise 2–1. Make a list of the characteristics of scientific knowledge. The list may help organize your thinking for other questions in this chapter.

_____

_____

_____

_____

_____

_____

_____

_____

Exercise 2–2.   The chapter mentions several characteristics of scientific knowledge. It also warns about confusing commonsense and casual observations with verified or potentially verifiable claims. In this exercise you will try to identify and differentiate between normative statements, which are statements that suggest how things *should* be, and empirical statements, which are statements that can be measured, tested, or verified through observation. For each of the following statements, decide if the statement is normative, empirical, a combination of the two, or if there is not enough information in the statement for you to decide. Write your responses in the space provided after each statement and briefly explain why you think your answer is correct.

a.   The Republicans won a majority of seats in the U.S. Senate in the 2014 midterm elections.

_____

_____

_____

_____

_____

b.   Offshore drilling should be banned in Alaska because it is immoral to risk damaging an otherwise pristine natural environment.

_____

_____

_____

_____

_____

c.   Early voting periods should be shortened because they disproportionately favor Democratic candidates for office.

_____

_____

_____

_____

_____

d.   Multiparty systems are better for representation than two-party systems.

_____

_____

_____

_____

_____

e. More people voted in the most recent election than in the previous election.

_____

_____

_____

_____

_____

f. Senior citizens are more likely to vote than college students.

_____

_____

_____

_____

_____

g. Scotland would be better off today if it had voted for independence in 2014.

_____

_____

_____

_____

_____

h. Freedom of religion is a fundamental right of all people.

_____

_____

_____

_____

_____

i. Democratic leaders always have better ideas on social policy than Republican leaders.

_____

_____

_____

_____

_____

j. Decriminalizing marijuana distribution and regulating sales can create a substantial source of tax revenue.[1]

_____

_____

_____

_____

_____

k. Too many people have been unable to find work.

_____

_____

_____

_____

_____

l. It doesn't make any sense to vote because so many ballots are cast in an election that no single vote is going to make a difference in the outcome.

_____

_____

_____

_____

_____

Exercise 2–3. Below are several paragraphs drawn from an article in which the author discusses a debate over how congressional districts are drawn:

I argue that map makers ought to "pack" districts with as many like-minded partisans as possible. Trying to draw "competitive districts" effectively cracks ideologically congruent votes into separate districts, which has the effect of increasing the absolute number of voters who will be unhappy with the outcome and dissatisfied with their representative.

One common objection to this method of districting [packing] is that it would add to the polarization in Congress by creating overwhelmingly Republican (Democratic) districts that are more likely to elect very conservative (liberal) members.

Some states, like Arizona, have passed laws or referenda specifying that a districting plan ought to maximize the number of competitive districts. This is not particularly surprising because the common

_____

[1] Kelley Phillips Erb, "It's No Toke: Colorado Pulls in Millions in Marijuana Tax Revenue," *Forbes*, March 11, 2014, http://www.forbes.com/sites/kellyphillipserb/2014/03/11/its-no-toke-colorado-pulls-in-millions-in-marijuana-tax-revenue/.

wisdom among most voters and certainly among the media is that the House of Representatives does not have enough competitive districts currently, and that an increase in the number of competitive elections or in the amount of turnover in Congress will somehow enhance representation.

From: Thomas L. Brunell, "Rethinking Redistricting: How Drawing Uncompetitive Districts Eliminates Gerrymanders, Enhances Representation, and Improves Attitudes toward Congress," *PS: Political Science and Politics* 40 (January 2006): 77–85.

a. Identify two normative statements or claims from the preceding text that can't be tested empirically as currently expressed.

_____

_____

_____

_____

_____

b. Write down three statements or claims in the preceding text that are empirical and can be tested.

_____

_____

_____

_____

_____

Exercise 2–4. Many people make the following claim: "You can't predict human behavior." In light of our discussion of the scientific approach to political science, do you find this claim to be valid? (*Hint:* Try breaking human behavior down into more specific traits or properties. For example, consider if people are naturally aggressive. Then think of ways that this might be empirically investigated.)

_____

_____

_____

_____

_____

_____

_____

Exercise 2–5.   Chapter 2 of the textbook highlights criticisms of the empirical study of political science. List the criticisms here.

_____

_____

_____

_____

_____

Which of the criticisms do you find most compelling and why?

_____

_____

_____

_____

_____

HELPFUL HINTS

Decoding the Ambiguity of Political Discourse

As we stated earlier, political discourse is frequently ambiguous, and you have to think carefully about what words really say. Sometimes a politician's meaning is clear. Consider President Obama's Rose Garden speech on a proposed nuclear deal with Iran.[2] In his speech, President Obama said, "The Islamic Republic of Iran has been advancing its nuclear program for decades," which was a straightforward factual statement that could be verified empirically. But he also claimed, "I made clear that we were prepared to resolve this issue diplomatically, but only if Iran came to the table in a serious way." The word *serious* makes this statement a judgment, not a factual proposition. Whether something is serious or not is an opinion. In some people's minds, Iran had been making serious attempts at diplomacy, but others thought differently. Who was right? It is hard to see how the proposition could be scientifically proven true or false.

[2] "Statement by the President on the Framework to Prevent Iran from Obtaining a Nuclear Weapon," April 2, 2015, www.whitehouse.gov/the-press-office/2015/04/02/statement-president-framework-prevent-iran-obtaining-nuclear-weapon.

Exercise 2–6. Chapter 2 in the textbook focuses on empirical research and using the scientific method. Empiricism is defined as "relying on observation to verify propositions." In this exercise you will want to consider *how* you might make observations to verify propositions. For each of the following empirical statements, indicate where you might look or how you might make observations to find information to verify the statement. In the example below, you will see that while you only need to provide one answer, there are many potential verification methods.

Example: A majority of voters oppose the use of the death penalty.

Answer: "I would search for survey results on national news organization Web sites," or "I would randomly sample students at my university and ask if they support the death penalty," or "I would call an interest group that focuses on the death penalty and ask about support for the death penalty among voters."

a. More voters are registered with the Democratic Party than the Republican Party in Pennsylvania.

    _____

b. The British Parliament currently has more than twelve parties represented by members.

    _____

c. Someone working forty hours a week and earning the minimum wage will still be below the federal poverty level for a family of two.

    _____

d. People are not willing to pay higher taxes to address climate change.

    _____

e. Texas has the most stringent voter identification law in the United States.

    _____

f. Ninety percent of deaths attributed to diarrheal diseases like cholera are children five years of age or younger.

    _____

Exercise 2–7. In order to think about the scientific components of empirical research, it is useful to compare research projects that are more scientific with projects that are less scientific. For this exercise you will select *two* examples of empirical research with publicly available results on the Internet.

The first step is to find two projects to compare. You should look for a project that closely adheres to the scientific method and a project that clearly does not. For example, you might search for a report or opinion poll from a commercial organization like Gallup or Roper, a news organization like the *New York Times* or NBC News, a research institution like Brookings or Cato, or a government agency like the Government Accounting Office or the Environmental Protection Agency. These sources are more likely to generate research projects that follow the scientific method. You might also consider projects produced by entertainment media companies like ESPN, US Weekly, or TMZ. These organizations are less likely to produce scientific research and should provide a clear contrast with more scientific work.

a. Identify the sources for the two projects you selected and briefly describe each project. Include the URLs where they can be found.

1. _____

_____

_____

2. _____

_____

_____

b. Compare and contrast the scientific nature of each project. Make sure to describe the scientific components each project made use of, such as random samples, replicability, generalization, etc.

_____

_____

_____

_____

_____

_____

_____

CHAPTER 3

Beginning the Research Process
Identifying a Research Topic, Developing Research Questions, and Reviewing the Literature

Probably everyone would agree that picking and narrowing a topic are the hardest tasks confronting a new researcher. One can, of course, easily identify issues worthy of research, such as the war on terror or the effects of television on democracy. But moving from a desire to "do something on _____" to a specific theme that can be researched with relatively few resources and little time can be quite challenging.

Part of the difficulty lies in having enough information about the subject matter. What is already known about it? How have previous investigators studied it? What important questions remain unanswered? All these considerations motivate the review of the literature.

Chapter 3 of the textbook provides readers with some insights and tips for conducting an effective literature review. It is particularly important that you understand the differences between different kinds of sources, such as scholarly and mass circulation publications.

We assume that everyone knows roughly how to surf the Internet. So these assignments mainly force students to think carefully about what they are looking for and finding. As mentioned in the textbook chapter, you can easily enough use Google or equivalent software to search for *terrorism* or *television* or any other subject. But these efforts are usually unsuccessful because they lead to too much irrelevant information. Instead we encourage the application of more specialized databases and library tools.

Exercise 3–1. For this exercise you will begin thinking about how to find a research question for a research paper. One potential source for ideas is a political news Web site. Visit an online political news organization like Politico.com or BBC.com. On the lines following, write six research questions based on political news stories from the organization you selected.

1. Research question: _____

   _____

2. Research question: _____

   _____

3. Research question: _____

   _____

4. Research question: _____

   _____

5. Research question: _____

    _____

6. Research question: _____

    _____

Exercise 3–2.   A potential source for research topic ideas is a political science journal. To complete this exercise you will need to find a copy of a political science journal, such as the *American Political Science Review*. Inside you will find a series of research articles. You should choose three articles that interest you. First, for each of the articles, identify the research question. (*Hint:* The research question is often found in the title, in an abstract, or in the first paragraph of the article.)

1. _____

2. _____

3. _____

Next, think about how you might investigate a similar topic to those found in each article you have chosen. Write down three new research questions below.

1. _____

2. _____

3. _____

Exercise 3–3.   Literature reviews are an important part of the research process. They provide the context and background so that a research project furthers our understanding of a political phenomenon by, among other things, attempting to resolve conflicting evidence, investigating a topic in different settings and populations, or using different measures of key concepts. Read the following excerpt of an article by David Niven.[1]

In reviewing the literature on the effects of negative campaign advertising, the author identifies several problems with the state of knowledge about the topic. What are these problems?

_____

_____

_____

_____

_____

_____

_____

_____

_____

---

[1] David Niven, "A Field Experiment on the Effects of Negative Campaign Mail on Voter Turnout in a Municipal Election," *Political Research Quarterly* 59, no. 2 (2006), 203–10. Excerpt from 203–5. Reprinted by permission of SAGE Publications Inc.

A Field Experiment on the Effects of Negative Campaign Mail on Voter Turnout in a Municipal Election

DAVID NIVEN, OHIO STATE UNIVERSITY

This field experiment is used to expose a random sample of voters in a 2003 mayoral race to various pieces of negative direct mail advertising. Exposure to the negative advertising stimulus improved turnout overall about 6 percent over that of the control group. Results show that different topics and amounts of negative advertising had different effects on turnout. The results suggest that alarm bells sounded by some previous research and by public officials may be overheated, because the effects of campaign negativity may not be monolithic, and it would appear political negativity can have a positive effect on turnout.

Is voter turnout subject to the effects of negative advertising? Political science research answers alternatively yes, no, or maybe. This study uses a field experiment in which voters in a mayoral contest were randomly exposed to negative campaign mail to assess the effects of negativity and move toward a better understanding of what has become a thoroughly confusing line of scholarship.

Indeed two of the most prominent studies on campaign advertising offer quite differing views on the effects of negativity. Ansolabehere and Iyengar (1995) conclude that negative ads directly result in lower voter turnout. Far from qualifying their results, Ansolabehere and Iyengar (1995:12) assert the evidence is definitive that negative campaign messages "pose a serious threat to democracy" and are "the single biggest cause" of public disdain for politics (2). By contrast, Green and Gerber (2004: 59) describe the effect of campaign advertising negativity as "slight." Depending on the circumstances, Green and Gerber find negativity modestly nudging turnout upwards or downwards. Far from labeling their results conclusive, however, Green and Gerber suggest much more work needs to be done to better understand negativity's effect.

While this study addresses Green and Gerber's call for continuing research on this question, studying the effects of campaign negativity is of value beyond simply satisfying an academic curiosity. Understanding the effects of negativity obviously has implications for how candidates, parties, and interest groups conduct campaigns. Moreover, various government bodies have expressed interest in some form of negative ad regulation. Legislative proposals have been introduced at the local, state, and national level to limit negative campaigning with measures such as forcing candidates to appear in their ads or subjecting political advertising copy to some form of official scrutiny. Indeed, "I would ban negative ads," says Senator John McCain (R-Arizona) of the legislation he would create if he could find a constitutional procedure to accomplish the task.[1] Thus, to understand negativity and its effects better is to become better armed to participate in a debate which pits the First Amendment against the very popular notion of cleaning up campaigns.

NEGATIVITY AND ITS EFFECTS

While there is no consensus definition of negative advertising, most researchers start with the notion that negativity involves the invoking of an opponent by a candidate (for example, Djupe and Peterson 2002). That is, a negative ad suggests the opponent should not be elected rather than that the sponsoring candidate should be elected. West (2001) defines a negative campaign ad as advertising that focuses at least 50 percent of its attention on the opponent rather than the sponsor of the ad. Such negativity may be focused on any aspect of the opponent's record, statements, campaign, or background.

Precise estimates vary, but there is no doubt that negativity occupies a significant place in the modern campaign advertising arsenal. In the 2000 presidential election, for example, content analyses of television commercials from the two parties' nominees found between half and 70 percent were negative (Benoit et al. 2003; West 2001). Other forms of communication, such as radio ads, were even more negatively oriented (Benoit et al. 2003). Looked at from another tack, researchers have found as few as 20 percent of ads directed purely toward extolling the virtues of the sponsoring candidate (Freedman and Lawton 2004).

Employing a variety of methods, researchers have produced intriguing results in studies of negativity effects. However, those results variously demonstrate the negative, positive, or lack of effect of negative advertising on voter turnout.

Negative Ads Alienate Citizens

Dating back at least to the Watergate era, political scientists have documented the capacity of the American public to become categorically dismissive of political leaders. That is, the untrustworthy behavior of one political figure can transcend the individual and come to represent the political class as a whole (Arterton 1974; Craig 1993; Miller 1974).

---

[1] Quoted in Jennifer Holland, "McCain vows to keep campaign clean no matter what," Associated Press Wire Service, December 22, 1999.

Political Research Quarterly, Vol. 59, No. 2 (June 2006): pp. 203–210

(Continued)

(Continued)

Consistent with that notion, researchers have found evidence that negative political advertising negatively affects recipients' feelings not only toward the target of the attack but also toward its sponsor (Basil, Schooler, and Reeves 1991; Lemert, Wanta, and Lee 1999; Garramone 1984; Merritt 1984; Roese and Sande 1993) and even toward politics more generally (Ansolabehere and Iyengar 1995; Ansolabehere, Iyengar, Simon, and Valentino 1994; Houston and Roskos-Ewoldsen 1998; Houston, Doan, and Roskos-Ewoldsen 1999).

Using various real world races, including senate, gubernatorial, and mayoral campaigns, Ansolabehere and Iyengar (1995) exposed subjects in a laboratory setting to campaign television ads of various tone. Participants in Ansolabehere and Iyengar's experiments who were shown a negative television ad were almost 5 percent less likely to report they planned on voting in the upcoming election than participants who were shown a positive ad. Those who saw negative ads were also less likely to express confidence in the political system, and less likely to express political efficacy. Ansolabehere and Iyengar conclude that negativity in politics is causing declining voter interest and participation.

According to other experimental studies, the capacity for negative ads to produce diffuse political negativity varies with the precise details of the ads. For example, Budesheim, Houston, and DePaola (1996) found that unsubstantiated negative attacks reduced respondents' ratings of both the attacker and the target. See also Shapiro and Rieger (1992). Other scholars have suggested that issue related attacks are more apt to be seen as fair game than attacks focused on personal characteristics (Johnson-Cartee and Copeland 1989; Roddy and Garramone 1988).

Nevertheless, there is a significant limitation in experimental laboratory work on this subject that is inherent to the method. For example, Ansolabehere and colleagues show subjects' campaign ads then inquire about their *intention* to vote. Various other experimental studies inquire about intentions to vote, or candidate preferences, but none is equipped to measure actual resulting behavior. Of course, there is no shortage of psychological research demonstrating the gaping chasm between knowing someone's intentions or preferences and knowing their actual resulting behavior; for example, Kaiser and Gutscher (2003). Moreover, political scientists have regularly documented the propensity of Americans to mislead researchers when they are asked about their voting habits; for example, Bernstein, Chadha, and Montjoy (2001). Thus, regardless of the rigor of the researchers or the ingenious nature of their design, the laboratory remains a difficult setting in which to demonstrate the effect of negative advertising on the real world behavior of turning out to vote.

Negative Ads Do Not Alienate Citizens

Meanwhile, other researchers posit that the effects of negativity might not be negative at all. Finkel and Geer (1998), for example, argue that negative ads stimulate turnout because they provide highly relevant information.

Indeed, researchers have attributed positive or stimulating effects to feelings of negativity as an explanation for some notable political phenomena. For example, some scholars conclude that one source of the typical midterm loss, in which the president's party generally loses House seats in elections without the presidency on the ballot, is that voters who are critical of the president have a higher motivation to participate than voters who are positively inclined toward the president (Kernell 1977).[2]

Contemporary evidence also suggests that reception of negative advertising may contribute to effective citizenry. Brians and Wattenberg (1996), using survey data, show that citizens who recalled seeing negative political advertising during the 1992 presidential election were more accurate in assessing candidates' overall issue positions in that election.[3] In fact, recalling ads was more closely associated with holding accurate assessments of the candidates than was regularly watching television news or reading a newspaper. West (2001), studying the content of the ad rather than the effects on recipients, similarly supports the notion of the value of negative advertising. West (2001: 69) finds "the most substantive appeals actually came in negative spots."

Consistent with this line of thinking, several studies have found links between campaign negativity and increased voter turnout (Lau and Pomper 2001; Djupe and Peterson 2002; Kahn and Kenney 1999; Finkel and Geer 1998; Wattenberg and Brians 1999). Based on survey results or aggregate trends, these studies are better able than laboratory experiments to demonstrate actual voter turnout, but are far weaker in demonstrating individual reception of negative ads and thus are less firmly able to demonstrate a causal link between receiving ads and deciding to vote.[4]

Given the limitations of both laboratory experiments and non-experimental approaches, a strong argument can be made for the need for field experiments to address negativity

---

[2] A variety of psychological studies suggest the potential for superficially "negative" messages to have a "positive" effect on behavior. The implications of several lines of research considering the effects of showing people the negatives of such behaviors as cigarette smoking (Grandpre et. al. 2003) and motorcycle riding (Bellaby and Lawrenson 2001) find that simply demonstrating negatives is not an effective strategy in preventing participation. Indeed, the negative messages may draw attention and interest, and ultimately augment willingness to participate.

[3] Some have argued that the implied causality is backwards. That is, remembering ads does not encourage clear thoughts on issues, but having clear thoughts on issues does encourage remembering ads. See, for example, Ansolabehere, Iyengar, and Simon (1999).

[4] There is a further concern in aggregate studies. If candidates use negativity strategically, as we have every reason to believe they do (Theilmann and Wilhite 1998), then an accurate measure of campaign negativity may be, in effect, a proxy for some other variable affecting turnout. For example, Djupe and Peterson's (2002) data suggest that the amount of negativity in the U.S. Senate primaries they studied rose with the number of quality candidates. They attribute the resulting higher turnout to the campaign negativity, but surely an equally strong case could be made that the presence of more quality candidates was the true source of the turnout increase.

effects. Field experiments offer internal validity (with random assignment and controlled exposure to the stimulus) and external validity (with diverse participants and a measurement of the actual resulting behavior).

Relatively few field experiments on negative advertising have been reported. Pfau and Kenski (1990) did use field experiments to assess the strategic value of negative campaign messages by exposing randomly chosen voters to independently created direct mail and push poll messages. More recently, Green and Gerber (2004) have employed field experiments to study a vast array of potential campaign influences on voter turnout. Among their studies have been two which included negative political advertising sent by mail.

Green and Gerber (2004) sent negative campaign mail to a sample of voters in a Connecticut mayoral election. Here both reception of the ad and actual voter turnout can be established, and the subjects include a random sample of potential voters. Green and Gerber found the effects of negative ads on turnout in the mayoral race were negative but quite small. In another contest, using the same basic design but different mailings, they found the effect of negative ads on turnout was small but positive. Green and Gerber (2004: 59) tentatively conclude that the effect of negative campaign mail on turnout is best understood as "slight."

Why do Ansolabehere and Iyengar (1995) find negativity an inherent threat to voter turnout while Green and Gerber (2004) find negativity has little relevance to turnout? Differences in methodology could explain the disparate conclusions. Ansolabehere and Iyengar (1995) used television to convey negative messages while Green and Gerber (2004)

used mail. However, nothing in Ansolabehere and Iyengar's (1995) theoretical approach suggests the effects of negativity require television as the medium of communication. Ansolabehere and Iyengar used a diverse but not random group of participants, while Green and Gerber (2004) used participants randomly drawn from several towns. However, nothing in Ansolabehere and Iyengar's (1995) protocol suggests they assembled a group of participants particularly attuned to the effects of negative messages. Probably the two most significant differences between the studies are that Ansolabehere and Iyengar's participants received their campaign communication in a laboratory, rather than in their homes (as was the case for Green and Gerber), and were asked about their intention to vote, rather than observed actually voting (as was the case for Green and Gerber). Both those factors might have contributed to an exaggeration of the negativity effect in Ansolabehere and Iyengar's study.[5] Beyond methodological differences, though, another compelling explanation exists. It is possible that both teams of researchers were measuring a realistic effect. That is, there may not be a monolithic negativity effect, and depending on the content of the ad and the circumstances of the race, negativity may in fact have quite varying effects on turnout.

Indeed, the confusing state of research in this area is well captured in Lau, Sigelman, Heldman, and Babbite's (1999) meta-analysis of studies on negative ads. After building a weighty dossier of studies, both published and unpublished, they found that previous research findings suggesting negative ads increase turnout are available in similar quantity to findings suggesting negative ads decrease turnout. This leaves the authors to conclude that the cumulative estimated effect of all these studies of negativity on turnout approaches zero. It is, in short, an area which demands replication with the best methodological approach: a randomized field experiment.

---

[5] Ansolabehere and colleagues dispute the notion that their techniques exaggerated the effect of negativity. Indeed, they label their estimate of negativity's effect as "conservative" (Ansolabehere, Iyengar, Simon, and Valentino 1994: 835).

Exercise 3–4. Suppose you are working as a research assistant for a professor of political science who is beginning a new book about the current state of income inequality in the United States. She needs to make sure that she has read as much serious analytic writing as possible and wants you to begin compiling a bibliography of published materials. Which of the following potential sources would you add to the list? Why? For each source below, indicate if it should be on the high priority list (a list of the most important analytic treatments) or on the low priority list (a list of less important sources). Explain your reasoning.

a. Economist Thomas Piketty's 2014 book *Capital in the Twenty-First Century*.

_____

_____

b. A 2013 National Public Radio interview with economist Tyler Cowan, author of *Average Is Over*.

_____

_____

c. Thomas Edsall's review in the *New York Times* of Joseph Stiglitz's 2012 book, *The Price of Inequality*.

_____

_____

d. A report titled "The Truth about Income Inequality," produced by the Center of the American Experiment.

_____

_____

e. A 2015 article titled "The Fiscal Disadvantage of Young Italians: A New View on Consolidation and Fairness," published in the *Journal of Economic Inequality*.

_____

_____

f. Jill Lepore's article, "Richer and Poorer, Accounting for Inequality," in *New Yorker* magazine.

_____

_____

g. A news article by Jim Siegel in the *Columbus Dispatch* about income inequality in Ohio titled "Income Gap Less in Ohio but Growing Everywhere."

_____

_____

h. A 2014 editorial in the *Washington Times* titled "Obama's 'Income Inequality' Deeper from Bailing out His Rich Wall Street Donors."

_____

_____

Exercise 3–5. Suppose you want to write a term paper or scholarly report on one of the following subjects: immigration policy in the United States, the nuclear nonproliferation treaty, the World Trade Organization, or climate change. Use one of these popular search engines—Google, Alltheweb, or Yahoo!—to begin building a bibliography.

a. Which search program did you choose?

_____

b. How many hits did your first search produce?

_____

c. How many sources on the *first* page of the search do you think would be helpful in writing an academic research report? Explain.

_____

_____

_____

_____

_____

d. Compile a brief bibliography—three citations for each of the following categories about your topic. See the textbook for a suggested format.

1. Articles in the mass media, such as newspapers and magazines

_____

_____

_____

_____

_____

_____

2. Essays, reports, and discussions published on the Internet or elsewhere by advocacy groups, not-for-profit organizations, and government agencies

_____

_____

_____

_____

_____

_____

3. Scholarly articles

_____

_____

_____

_____

_____

_____

e. Now conduct a search using the other search engines. Do these search engines generally locate the same sources, or are there important differences in what each finds? Which do you prefer? Why? And, more importantly, do you see the need to limit a topic?

_____

_____

_____

_____

_____

_____

_____

_____

Exercise 3–6.   In this exercise you will examine a research article with respect to its citations to learn how to find related work. Literature reviews can be completed much more quickly if you can efficiently find research related to your topic of study. Imagine that you are interested in researching how people connect through social associations. You begin by finding one article written by Kwak, Shah, and Holbert that is directly related to your topic. You should find the article in the Social Science Citation index (also known as Web of Science) or Google Scholar using this citation: Nojin Kwak, Dhavan V. Shah, and R. Lance Holbert, "Connecting, Trusting, and Participating: The Direct and Interactive Effects of Social Associations," *Political Research Quarterly* 57, no. 4 (2004): 643–52. Now answer the questions below and think about how each answer could help you find additional materials for your own project.

a. How many sources did this article cite?

_____

b. What kind of sources were cited, and in what fields of study were the citations located?

_____

_____

_____

c. Click on each author's name. How many citations are listed for each? Do the topics of other work related to the article you are investigating appear? What evidence did you use to make this judgment?

_____

_____

_____

d. How many times has this article been cited?

_____

_____

e. What kinds of work were cited in this article, and in what fields of study were the citations located?

_____

_____

_____

Exercise 3–7.   Use Web of Science or Google Scholar to search for articles related to one of the following topics:

1. Do harsh penalties have any effect on illegal drug use?
2. Is the South more politically conservative than other regions?
3. The role of civic culture in democracy
4. Why do some states enact laws against gay marriage?
5. Immigration to the United States from Latin America

Using an acceptable format, list your first five sources here.

1. _____

2. _____

3. _____

4. _____

5. _____

Exercise 3–8.   Suppose you are interning with your state's Office of the Attorney General. Your boss is interested in reviewing scientific evidence about the potential negative effects of voter identification laws because your state legislature is considering making the state's voter identification laws more stringent. Your task is to find relevant political science research articles that can help inform your boss on the topic. Use the search engine of your choice to find six articles published in political science journals. List the citations below.

1. _____

2. _____

3. _____

4. _____

5. _____

6. _____

HELPFUL HINTS

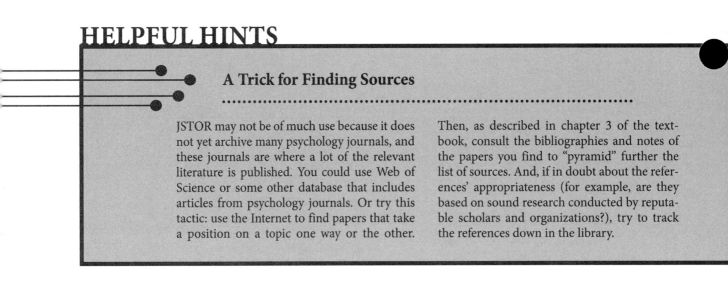

A Trick for Finding Sources

JSTOR may not be of much use because it does not yet archive many psychology journals, and these journals are where a lot of the relevant literature is published. You could use Web of Science or some other database that includes articles from psychology journals. Or try this tactic: use the Internet to find papers that take a position on a topic one way or the other.

Then, as described in chapter 3 of the textbook, consult the bibliographies and notes of the papers you find to "pyramid" further the list of sources. And, if in doubt about the references' appropriateness (for example, are they based on sound research conducted by reputable scholars and organizations?), try to track the references down in the library.

Exercise 3–9. Sharpen your literature review skills by finding and listing six articles that rely primarily, or to some degree, on randomized experiments. A specific database such as JSTOR will be most rewarding. But here is a tip that can be applied to just about any kind of search: read *abstracts* when available instead of trying to skim entire articles. Using a correct format, list the results of your search here.

1. _____

2. _____

3. _____

4. _____

5. _____

6. _____

Exercise 3–10. If you know of scholars who have conducted research on a topic of interest—perhaps you have culled names from the bibliographies in textbooks—you can search for their Web pages. Frequently these pages will provide a curriculum vitae or list of publications, some of which may be in electronic form. Using the name of an author of an article or book listed on one of your syllabi from a political science course, search for the author's Web page and print out his or her curriculum vitae or list of publications.

CHAPTER 4

The Building Blocks of Social Scientific Research
Hypotheses, Concepts, and Variables

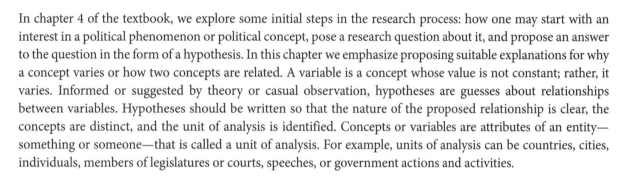

In chapter 4 of the textbook, we explore some initial steps in the research process: how one may start with an interest in a political phenomenon or political concept, pose a research question about it, and propose an answer to the question in the form of a hypothesis. In this chapter we emphasize proposing suitable explanations for why a concept varies or how two concepts are related. A variable is a concept whose value is not constant; rather, it varies. Informed or suggested by theory or casual observation, hypotheses are guesses about relationships between variables. Hypotheses should be written so that the nature of the proposed relationship is clear, the concepts are distinct, and the unit of analysis is identified. Concepts or variables are attributes of an entity— something or someone—that is called a unit of analysis. For example, units of analysis can be countries, cities, individuals, members of legislatures or courts, speeches, or government actions and activities.

Exercise 4–1. Chapter 4 focuses on the construction of hypotheses. In this exercise you will assess the research question below and generate hypotheses you would want to test.

a. In the space provided, write six hypotheses you would want to test to answer the question provided. In writing your hypotheses pay close attention to the six characteristics of a good hypothesis as discussed in the textbook: (1) empirical, (2) general, (3) plausible, (4) specific, (5) stated as intended for testing, (6) testable. Also, try to generate hypotheses that include different dependent variables related to the research question. For example, consider different kinds of political participation that may have different motivating factors (independent variables).

Research Question: Why do citizens participate in politics?

1. _____

_____

2. _____

_____

3. _____

_____

4. _____

_____

5. _____

    _____

6. _____

    _____

b. Specify the unit of analysis for your research question and hypotheses. (*Hint:* The unit of analysis should be consistent across the question, theory, and hypotheses.)

    _____

    _____

HELPFUL HINTS

Identifying Variables and Units of Analysis

An empirical hypothesis has three distinct components: the unit of analysis, the independent variable, and the dependent variable. First, remember that the particular type of actor whose political behavior is named in a hypothesis is the unit of analysis for the research project. Second, remember that independent variables are the measurements of the phenomena that are thought to *influence, affect,* or *cause* some other phenomenon. A dependent variable is thought *to be caused, to depend upon,* or *to be a function of* an independent variable. Finally, something cannot be both a unit of analysis and a variable. Something cannot be both an independent and a dependent variable.

Exercise 4–2.   In this exercise you will consider the difference between variables and a unit of analysis. You will find below a series of hypotheses. For each hypothesis identify the independent variable, the dependent variable, and the unit of analysis. When doing so, keep in mind the following:

Example: An increase in a person's education causes an increase in a person's income.

Answer: Independent variable: education; dependent variable: income; unit of analysis: individuals

a. The U.S. public is more willing to support the use of the country's military forces when U.S. interests are affected than when they are not.

    _____

b. An increase in the number of nongovernmental organizations active in a nondemocratic country increases that country's likelihood of moving to a democratic form of government.

    _____

c. States with more counties spend more money on law enforcement than states with fewer counties.

    _____

d. Increases in international aid to improve water quality cause marked improvement in public health in developing countries.

_____

e. Registered Republicans were more likely to vote in the 2014 midterm election than registered Democrats.

_____

f. Elections that take place during warm weather will have higher turnout than elections that take place during cold weather.

_____

Exercise 4–3. Each of the following hypotheses is faulty in some way. Some do not specify the relationship between the variables (correlation or causation), some do not specify the direction of the relationship (positive or negative), and some are too specific, tautological, or normative or simply do not make sense. Rewrite an improved hypothesis on the line below each hypothesis.

a. There is a correlation between the president's approval rating and the price of gasoline.

_____

_____

b. Higher recidivism rates and the availability of drug treatment programs in prisons might be related in some way.

_____

_____

c. The turnout rate in my legislative district was low because the incumbent ran unopposed.

_____

_____

d. Cities with high rates of public transit ridership are better than cities in which ridership is low.

_____

_____

e. The more miles of coastline that a country has, the less likely it is to have a federal system of government.

_____

_____

f. People who are active in politics tend to contribute money to election campaigns more often than people who are not active in politics.

_____

_____

Exercise 4–4. For each pair of variables write a hypothesis that defines the relationship between the variables (correlation or causation) and the direction of the relationship.

a. Interest in politics; likelihood of voting

_____

b. Number of gun-related deaths; strength of gun laws

_____

c. Money spent on abstinence programs; number of teenage pregnancies

_____

d. Time devoted to civil rights in the State of the Union address; number of civil rights bills introduced in Congress

_____

e. Corporate income tax rate; number of new businesses

_____

Exercise 4–5. Below are sets of three variables. On the lines after each set, do the following:

- Write a hypothesis relating the first two variables.
- Identify independent and dependent variables.
- State how you expect the third variable to affect the hypothesized relationship.
- Draw an arrow diagram including all three variables.
- Determine whether the third variable is antecedent, intervening, or alternative.

a. Primary caregiver for children (primary caregiver, not primary caregiver); support for Family Medical Leave Law (thermometer scale for support); gender (female, male).

_____

_____

_____

b. Intention to vote in upcoming election; respondent's general interest in politics; predicted outcome of election ("too close to call," "somewhat competitive," "lopsided victory")

_____

_____

_____

c. Type of lightbulb purchased (regular, energy efficient); difference in cost of regular and high-efficiency lightbulbs (small difference, large difference); concern about global climate change

_____

_____

_____

Exercise 4–6. Write a research question that uses each of the following units of analysis:

a. Individuals

_____

b. Countries

_____

c. Laws

_____

d. Groups

_____

e. Organizations

_____

CHAPTER 5

The Building Blocks of Social Scientific Research
Measurement

Measurement involves deciding how to measure the presence, absence, or number of concepts in a research project. Reliability and validity of measures are key concerns.

A reliable measure yields a consistent, stable result as long as the concept being measured remains unchanged. Measurement strategies that rely on memories, for example, may be quite unreliable because the ability to remember specific information may vary depending on when the measurement is made and whether distractions are present.

Valid measures correspond well with the meaning of the concept being measured. Researchers often develop rather elaborate schemes to measure complex concepts.

Level of measurement is an important aspect of a measurement scheme. There are four levels of measurement. From lowest to highest, these levels are as follows: nominal, ordinal, interval, and ratio. Choosing the appropriate statistics for the analysis of data depends on knowing the level of measurement of your variables. Frequently a variable can be measured using a variety of schemes. Choosing the scheme that uses the highest level of measurement possible provides the most information and is the most precise measure of a concept. Researchers frequently recode data, thus changing the level of measurement of a variable.

HELPFUL HINTS

Recoding Data

....

There are two strategies for recoding data to combine or collapse categories of a measure:

1. **Theoretical**. Choose categories that are meaningfully distinct, where theory would tell you that the differences between the categories are important or where you can see that there are distinct clusters of scores or values. For example, when combining actual household income amounts into income levels, a researcher might consider what the official poverty level is and group all households with incomes below that level into the lowest income group.

2. **Equally Sized Categories**. Choose categories so that each category has roughly an equal number of cases. In addition, limit the number of categories so that each category has at least ten cases.

Exercise 5–1. What is the level of measurement of the following measures? If you think there could be more than one level of measurement, explain your answer.

a. Type of government system (authoritarian, communist, democracy, monarchy, other)

_____

_____

b. Number of vetoes issued by each president of the United States

_____

_____

c. Race (Asian, Black, Hispanic, White, other)

_____

_____

d. Hours spent on social media per day (0-1, 2-3, 4 or more)

_____

_____

e. Literacy rate in each country (percentage literate)

_____

_____

f. State uses the death penalty (yes, no)

_____

_____

g. Number of witnesses in a Senate committee hearing

_____

_____

h. Political ideology (very conservative, conservative, moderate, liberal, very liberal)

_____

_____

i. Party identification (Democrat, Republican, Independent, other, none)

_____

_____

j. Number of border countries

_____

_____

k. Member of U.S. Chamber of Commerce (yes, no)

_____

_____

l. Year first elected to public office

_____

_____

m. Primary policy objective of military intervention (foreign policy restraint, humanitarian intervention, internal political change)

_____

_____

n. Tone of campaign commercial (positive, mixed, negative)

_____

_____

o. Year in college (freshman, sophomore, junior, senior)

_____

_____

p. Health care system (government-managed health care, health care coverage required by law, private health care system)

_____

_____

Exercise 5–2. Levels of measurement are important because they serve as a way to think about both the amount of information available in a measure and the mathematical properties of the measure. In this exercise you are going to consider the amount of information available in variables that measure the same concept with different levels of measurement. For each of the variables below, identify the level of measurement. Second, explain why one variable provides more information than the other. Finally, why might you prefer to use one measure over the other? Why is capturing more information important?

Concept: Education

Variable #1:

What is your highest completed level of education?

1. No formal education
2. Elementary school
3. Middle school
4. High school
5. College
6. Advanced degree

Variable #2:

How many years of formal education have you completed?

_____

_____

_____

_____

Exercise 5–3. Herrmann, Tetlock, and Visser define the disposition of military assertiveness as "the inclination toward different methods of defending American interests abroad, in particular, whether a person prefers more militant and assertive strategies or more accommodative and cooperative approaches."[1] To measure military assertiveness, they used ten items. For the first eight items, they asked respondents to indicate whether they strongly agreed, agreed, neither agreed nor disagreed, disagreed, or strongly disagreed with the statement.

Which of the following items do you think are the most valid measures of the concept of military assertiveness and why? Which ones do you have trouble relating to the concept and why? What kind of validity (face or construct) do you think the items exhibit?

1. The best way to ensure world peace is through American military strength.
2. The use of military force only makes problems worse.
3. Rather than simply reacting to our enemies, it's better for us to strike first.
4. Generally, the more influence America has with other nations, the better off they are.

---

[1] Richard K. Herrmann, Philip E. Tetlock, and Penny S. Visser, "Mass Public Decisions to Go to War: A Cognitive-Interactionist Framework," *American Political Science Review* 93 (September 1999): 554.

5. People can be divided into two distinct classes: the weak and the strong.
6. The facts on crime, sexual immorality, and the recent public disorders all show that we have to crack down harder on troublemakers if we are going to save our moral standards and preserve law and order.
7. Obedience and respect for authority are the most important virtues children should learn.
8. Although at times I may not agree with the government, my commitment to the United States always remains strong.
9. When you see the American flag flying, does it make you feel extremely good, somewhat good, or not very good?
10. How important is military defense spending to you personally: very important, important, or not at all important?

Most valid measures of the concept of military assertiveness:

_____

_____

_____

_____

Worst "fit" for concept:

_____

_____

_____

Kind of validity:

_____

_____

_____

_____

Exercise 5–4. Suppose you think that moral values are theoretically important in explaining voting behavior. Before you can write your theory or test your hypotheses involving moral values, you must conceptualize and operationalize the concept. In the space following, conceptualize (define the term) and operationalize (decide how you will record the quantitative variable) moral values.

Conceptualization: _____

_____

_____

Operationalization: _____

_____

_____

_____

_____

_____

Exercise 5–5. Operationalization is deciding how to record empirical observations of the occurrence of an attribute or a behavior using numerals or scores. In other words, it is deciding how to move from defined concept to quantifiable variable. In this exercise you are going to consider the challenges involved in quantifying both concrete and abstract concepts that are commonly used in political science research. You will find below a series of conceptualized terms. Your job is to explain how you would operationalize each term for use in a survey research project by creating the questions that would yield the appropriate variable for each concept. (*Hint:* Concrete terms are much easier to work with than abstract terms. Pay close attention to the abstract terms, such as *ideology* and *efficacy*.)

Example: Voter registration: Whether someone is currently registered to vote.

Answer: Ask each respondent to indicate whether he or she is currently registered to vote by asking, "Are you currently registered to vote in your state?" (1) Yes, I am registered to vote; (0) No, I am not registered to vote.

a.   Gender: Male and female

_____

_____

_____

b.   Household income: The amount of money earned by all members of a household in a year

_____

_____

_____

c.   Race: The race each respondent most closely identifies with

_____

_____

_____

d. Ideology: A set of beliefs and ideas, including one's moral code and worldview. The most important issues and ideas involve how the government should address those unable to provide food, health care, and housing for themselves and their children. The extent to which the government should extend services to support those in need in these areas makes up the worldview.

_____

_____

_____

e. Political efficacy: The belief that one's political action will have a meaningful effect. In particular I define political action as interpersonal communication with elected officials.

_____

_____

_____

Exercise 5–6. Table 5–1 contains a frequency distribution of senators' scores on the American Federation of Labor–Congress of Industrial Organizations (AFL–CIO) rating system for 2005. The left-hand column shows the actual scores given to senators; the columns to the right show how many senators received the scores. Suppose you wanted to code these data into an *ordinal-level measure* with *two categories*. What are *two ways* this could be done? Give the range of scores that would fall into the categories in your ordinal-level measures.

First ordinal-level measure: _____

_____

_____

_____

Second ordinal-level measure: _____

_____

_____

_____

Exercise 5–7. Table 5–2 shows the distribution of the average index scores of each state's delegation to the U.S. House of Representatives on the League of Conservation Voters (LCV) index for 2006. The index ranges from 0 to 100 and represents the percentage of times that a member voted in favor of the LCV position on selected issues. Suppose that you wanted to group the average state delegation scores into *four categories* for a

TABLE 5–1
AFL–CIO 2005 Senators' Rating Scores

Score	Frequency	Percentage	Cumulative Percentage
0	1	1.0	1.0
7	16	16.0	17.0
8	1	1.0	18.0
14	19	19.0	37.0
15	2	2.0	39.0
17	1	1.0	40.0
21	6	6.0	46.0
23	1	1.0	47.0
29	3	3.0	50.0
46	1	1.0	51.0
50	1	1.0	52.0
57	3	3.0	55.0
64	1	1.0	56.0
69	1	1.0	57.0
71	3	3.0	60.0
77	2	2.0	62.0
79	10	10.0	72.0
85	1	1.0	73.0
86	7	7.0	80.0
92	3	3.0	83.0
93	8	8.0	91.0
100	9	9.0	100.0
Total	100	100.0	

Source: American Federation of Labor–Congress of Industrial Organizations (AFL–CIO), 2005.

new variable called "Support for LCV." What range of values would be included in each of the categories? Justify your answer.

_____

_____

_____

_____

TABLE 5–2

League of Conservation Voters 2006
State Delegation Averages for the House

Score	Frequency	Percentage	Cumulative Percentage
0	3	6.0	6.0
4	1	2.0	8.0
5	1	2.0	10.0
9	1	2.0	12.0
14	1	2.0	14.0
19	1	2.0	16.0
20	2	4.0	20.0
22	2	4.0	24.0
25	1	2.0	26.0
26	1	2.0	28.0
27	2	4.0	32.0
32	1	2.0	34.0
36	1	2.0	36.0
37	1	2.0	38.0
38	2	4.0	42.0
39	4	8.0	50.0
40	1	2.0	52.0
42	1	2.0	54.0
45	1	2.0	56.0
47	1	2.0	58.0
50	2	4.0	62.0
52	1	2.0	64.0
54	1	2.0	66.0
61	1	2.0	68.0
62	1	2.0	70.0
67	3	6.0	76.0
68	1	2.0	78.0
75	1	2.0	80.0
77	1	2.0	82.0
78	2	4.0	86.0
83	1	2.0	88.0
85	1	2.0	90.0
88	2	4.0	94.0
89	1	2.0	96.0
99	1	2.0	98.0
100	1	2.0	100.0
Total	100	100.0	

Source: League of Conservation Voters index, 2006.

Exercise 5–8. Below you will find a series of hypotheses. For each hypothesis identify the variables you would need to test the hypothesis and explain how you could measure each variable. When explaining your measurement strategy, be careful to consider validity and reliability.

a. Small business owners are more likely to support tax cuts than other voters.

_____

_____

_____

_____

_____

b. The availability of government-subsidized child care causes household income to rise.

_____

_____

_____

_____

_____

c. An increase in the number of nongovernmental organizations operating in an authoritarian state increases the rate at which the state democratizes.

_____

_____

_____

_____

_____

d. Access to clean drinking water causes life expectancy to increase.

_____

_____

_____

_____

_____

_____

_____

CHAPTER 6

Research Design
Making Causal Inferences

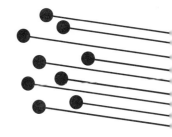

Chapter 6 of the textbook has two major goals. The first is to emphasize the importance of thinking through a research question in order to find methods and data that will illuminate the issue. The second is to describe an "ideal" standard of evidence against which results can be judged and to suggest some ways that researchers can strive to reach that level of verification.

On the surface, political scientists engage in all sorts of activities, few of which may look like causal analysis. But in that part of the discipline that thinks of itself as "scientific," a major goal is the search for verifiable causal relationships.

We began the chapter by showing what is necessary to demonstrate causality and explaining how hard it is to do so. We also argued that the randomized experiment provides a model for supporting causal claims. Unfortunately, as powerful as they are, true experiments are neither feasible nor ethical in many research contexts, so we suggested alternative designs that might be called *approximations to experiments*. By that phrase we mean procedures that accomplish roughly the same things as random assignment of subjects, physical manipulation and control of the test factor and experimental environment, and direct observation of measurement of behavior. But these procedures do so indirectly and most often with statistics.

Most of the following assignments call for serious thought rather than paper-and-pencil calculations. The purpose is to ensure that some of the basic ideas are clearly understood. We do not expect that most students will be able to design and carry out a major empirical research project. At the same time, it is important to understand how systematic and rigorous research proceeds.

Exercise 6–1.   Sometimes political science students can be confused by similar-sounding terms, such as *civil liberties* and *civil rights*, or terms that describe similar but distinct concepts, such as *slander* and *libel*. This confusion is often exacerbated when it comes to methodological terms. This exercise is about reinforcing your understanding of similar terms. For each of the word pairs below, define each term and then explain the important differences between them.

a.   Internal validity and external validity

_____

_____

_____

b. Causation and correlation

_____

_____

_____

c. Experimental effect and experimental group

_____

_____

_____

d. Test factor and pretest

_____

_____

_____

e. Experiment and field experiment

_____

_____

_____

HELPFUL HINTS

Think About the Question

You do not need to know much about the Supreme Court to complete this exercise. First, reread the section in chapter 1 titled "A Look into Judicial Decision Making and Its Effects." Then, identify and list some of the variables or factors that are supposed to influence justices' opinions. (An obvious example is the degree to which a justice strictly adheres to legal principles, but the literature cited in the text mentions many others.) Finally, think about how these variables might be interconnected. Which of the connections would you call causal? Which are spurious?

Exercise 6–2. Chapter 1 brings up an important point about the judicial system in the United States. Recall that Jeffrey A. Segal and Albert D. Cover in one study and Jeff Yates and Andrew Whitford in another looked at how or on what grounds Supreme Court justices decide cases.[1] In particular, they asked whether justices render opinions solely on the basis of legal precedents and the application of law or whether other factors enter into the process. In the space following, draw three different diagrams that represent causal, spurious,

[1] Jeffrey A. Segal and Albert D. Cover, "Ideological Values and the Votes of U.S. Supreme Court Justices," *American Political Science Review* 83 (June 1989): 557–65; and Jeff Yates and Andrew Whitford, "Presidential Power and the United States Supreme Court," *Political Research Quarterly* 51 (June 1998): 539–50.

and alternative propositions about judicial decision making. Also provide a short explanation of what the diagrams mean.

_____

_____

_____

Exercise 6–3. List the strengths and weaknesses of randomized controlled experiments. In particular, pay attention to the important concepts raised in the chapter, including internal and external validity.

a. Strengths:

_____

_____

_____

_____

_____

_____

b. Weaknesses:

_____

_____

_____

_____

_____

Exercise 6–4.   An investigator wanted to know if repeated and prolonged exposure to pro-life videos could change opinions about abortion policy. He drew a random sample of 100 people from the community of Nowhere and assigned them to one of four groups. The first twenty-five men to appear were assigned to group 1; the rest of the men were then placed in group 2. The first twenty-five women were assigned to group 3, and the remaining women went to group 4. (Groups 2 and 4 may have had unequal numbers, but just ignore this possibility when answering.) The "treatments" were as follows:

Group 1 (Experimental):   Over a period of three days, the twenty-five male participants viewed thirty minutes per day of anti-abortion commercials.

Group 2 (Control):   Over a period of three days, the remaining males watched thirty minutes per day of automobile television advertisements and then went home.

Group 3 (Experimental):   Over a period of three days, the twenty-five females watched the same anti-abortion ads as the men for thirty minutes per day.

Group 4 (Control):   Over a period of three days, the remaining females watched thirty minutes per day of automobile commercials and then went home.

The subjects' attitudes about abortion policy were measured at the time they were assigned to a group *and* one week after the last treatment had been administered. For the two experimental groups, the measurements showed a large decrease in support for any kind of legal abortion. The control subjects did not change their views very much.

After collecting and analyzing all the data, the researcher arrived at two conclusions. First, exposure to persuasive messages does change opinions. In this case, the ads made both men and women less likely to support abortion rights. Second, the effect of the messages was exactly the same for men and women.

What do you think of this research design? In particular, answer the following questions:

a.   Assume that the research design is sound. To what population, if any, can the results be generalized? (Write "yes" or "no" and a comment if you wish.)

  1.   The people of Nowhere
  2.   Only the men of Nowhere
  3.   Only those people with heavy exposure to anti-abortion ads
  4.   Men and women in the United States

b.   What is external validity? In this context, which of these statements about external validity is correct?

  1.   Men and women in the United States react similarly to persuasive communications in general.
  2.   Men and women in the United States react similarly to the kinds of anti-abortion ads presented in the experiment.
  3.   Men and women in Nowhere react similarly to these type of persuasive messages.
  4.   Public opinion on political issues is affected by television communications.

c.   Now go back to the design as presented. Is it sound? Which of the following research standards and principles seem to be violated? Explain.

Random sampling

_____

_____

_____

_____

Creation of a control group

_____

_____

_____

_____

Demand characteristics

_____

_____

_____

_____

Experimental mortality

_____

_____

_____

_____

Exercise 6–5.   This item is a question for discussion and study.

Imagine that you have been granted immediate graduation from your school. Congratulations! You have also landed a very good job as an advisor to the president. The president is facing budget trouble and wants to know how voters will react to three policy proposals: a tax hike, a tax cut, or leaving tax rates unchanged. It is your job to decide upon a research design or strategy that would best suit the problem.

What you want to know is how public support for the president will change over time if taxes are cut, raised, or left at the status quo. Briefly answer the following questions: What type of research design would give you the best internal or external validity? How could you demonstrate that your results were reliable? What are the relative advantages of using a survey and an experiment? Would a small-N design, such as a case study or a focus group, be useful? Why or why not?

_____

_____

_____

_____

_____

_____

_____

_____

_____

_____

_____

Exercise 6–6. Imagine that your professor mentions in class that most college students rely on the *Daily Show* for political news and information. Your professor seems to think that following politics is necessary to get many of the jokes but that no one really learns anything by watching the show. You have decided to test your professor's ideas in the form of a research project for class.

In the space below, state the research question and hypotheses you intend to test as clearly and succinctly as possible. Next, explain how you would test these hypotheses and evaluate the strengths and weaknesses of this research strategy.

_____

_____

_____

_____

_____

_____

_____

_____

_____

Exercise 6–7. For each of the following research questions, describe the design or strategy you would propose to investigate the issue. Note that although you do not have to conduct the investigation, you should make your design as practical as possible. Devise a strategy that you feel would maximize the "scientific" payoff.

a. How did President Obama affect the outcome of the 2014 congressional elections?

_____

_____

_____

_____

_____

_____

b. How did the increase in the number of earthquakes in Oklahoma between 2009 and 2015 affect fracking practices in the state?

_____

_____

_____

_____

_____

c. How did Prime Minister Benjamin Netanyahu's speech at the United States Capitol in 2015 affect the 2015 Israeli election?

_____

_____

_____

_____

_____

d. How does malaria affect the length of civil wars?

_____

_____

_____

_____

_____

e. What is the effect of ballot position on voter choice in a city election in which there are no incumbents and no party labels?

_____

_____

_____

_____

_____

f. Do early education programs, such as Head Start, improve educational outcomes for enrolled children?

_____

_____

_____

_____

_____

g. What was the reaction of the leadership of the Mexican political party PRI (Partido de la Revolución Democrática) to the passage of the North American Free Trade Agreement?

_____

_____

_____

_____

_____

h. How do Super PACs affect presidential primary elections?

_____

_____

_____

_____

_____

Exercise 6–8. There are many political science research questions that could be addressed with multiple research designs. Consider, for example, the politics around climate change. One could try to explain why citizens, lawmakers, or bureaucrats hold various opinions about the causes of or solutions for climate change. One might also investigate the effectiveness of various government efforts in dealing with climate change.

a. How might you use a cross-sectional research design to study the politics of climate change? (*Hint:* You might consider using a respondent's opinion about a climate change issue as a dependent variable.)

_____

_____

_____

_____

_____

b. How might you use a longitudinal or time series research design to study the politics of climate change? (*Hint:* You might consider using a measure of the effect of climate change, such as CO_2 levels, over time as your dependent variable.)

_____

_____

_____

_____

_____

_____

_____

_____

Exercise 6-9. For this assignment you will first need to read Richard Fenno's 1977 article, "U.S. House Members in Their Constituencies: An Exploration," *American Political Science Review* 71: 883–917. You will want to pay special attention to the first ten to twelve pages. As you will see, in this article Fenno relied on a participant observation research design (see chapter 8). For this exercise consider and describe how you could test Fenno's conclusions with an alternative research design.

a. What type of research design would you use?

_____

_____

_____

b. What are the advantages and disadvantages of this research design relative to Fenno's design?

_____

_____

_____

c. How would you operationalize a home style?

_____

_____

_____

Exercise 6–10.   For this assignment you will first need to read Stephen D. Ansolabehere, Shanto Iyengar, Adam Simon, and Nicholas Valentino's article, "Does Attack Advertising Demobilize the Electorate?," *American Political Science Review* 88, no. 4 (1994): 829–38. You will want to pay special attention to the first three pages and appendix A. This exercise asks you to contemplate the authors' experimental research design and answer the questions below.

a. What is the research question?

_____

b. Please summarize the theory.

_____

_____

_____

c. What is the central hypothesis the authors want to test?

_____

d. In the literature review the authors point out limitations in previous work on this topic. What were those limitations and why are they important in terms of internal validity?

_____

_____

_____

e. What special design features did the authors use to improve on the limitations of previous work?

_____

_____

_____

f. How did the authors address external validity through their nonrandom sampling methods? Why is this important?

_____

_____

_____

CHAPTER 7

Sampling

The attempt to verify statements empirically lies at the core of modern political science. Abstract theorizing is a valuable, even necessary, activity. Still, most social scientists feel that at some point theories have to "face reality." Thus, as we have seen in several chapters (such as chapters 4, 5, and 6), carefully observing and collecting data is an integral part of the research process.

Unfortunately, in all too many situations it is not possible to observe each member of a population. Hence, sampling—the process of drawing a small set of cases from a larger population—becomes necessary.

The social sciences depend heavily on sampling. This fact sometimes troubles the general public. "How," many citizens ask, "can you make a claim about all the 322 million people in the United States when you've interviewed just five hundred of them?" Some people, however, including many reporters, politicians, and political advisers, act as though polling is an exact science. Chapter 7 addresses these issues.

More specifically, sampling raises two questions. First, *how* should the subset of observations be collected from the population, and, second, *how reliable and valid* are inferences made on the basis of a sample? The first question pertains to sample types or designs, whereas the second deals with statistics and probability.

At this level of your training it is not possible to go into detail about either question. But if you work through these assignments you may begin to get a feel for the basics of sampling techniques and their properties. None of this involves any mathematical sophistication, but it does require careful thought.

Exercise 7–1. Sometimes students can be confused by terms that describe similar but distinctly different concepts. This confusion is often exacerbated when it comes to methodological terms. This exercise is about reinforcing your understanding of similar terms. For each of the word pairs below, define each term and then explain the important differences between them.

a. Population parameter and estimator

_____

_____

_____

b. Sampling frame and sampling unit

_____

_____

_____

c. Element and stratum

_____

_____

_____

d. Probability sample and nonprobability sample

_____

_____

_____

e. Proportionate and disproportionate sample

_____

_____

_____

_____

Exercise 7–2. Generally, political scientists prefer to use probability samples whenever possible to make causal inferences. In this exercise you will consider how you might make use of nonprobability sampling methods. The text describes four kinds of random sampling technique (simple random sample, systematic sample, stratified sample, cluster sample) and four nonprobability sampling techniques (purposive, convenience, quota, and snowball). Below you will find a description of eight samples. Label each example with the sampling technique listed above that best matches the example.

a. Selecting every twentieth person who exits a polling station to interview him or her about vote choices

_____

b. Hand-selecting participants in an experiment based on race, gender, and education level so that the sample mirrors the population on those three characteristics

_____

c. Asking a neighbor who homeschools her children about her opinion on state education policy then asking for additional homeschoolers' contact information to find more participants for the study

_____

d. Randomly selecting Florida and Ohio from all fifty states; randomly selecting Miami-Dade County and Franklin County from a list of all counties in Florida and Ohio; and randomly selecting 750 respondents in Miami-Dade County, Florida, and randomly selecting 750 respondents in Franklin County, Ohio

_____

e. Drawing counties at random from a list of all counties in California to examine the effects of water policy on water usage

f. A professor asking the 135 members of her class to complete a survey on political attitudes

g. Randomly selecting 72 percent of a sample from a list of male legislators and 28 percent of a sample from a list of female legislators

h. Choosing the Washington, Lincoln, F. D. Roosevelt, and Johnson presidencies as cases to study the president at war because they are the most interesting cases

Exercise 7–3. The following is an excerpt from an article by Laura Beth Nielsen titled "Situating Legal Consciousness: Experiences and Attitudes of Ordinary Citizens about Law and Street Harassment."[1] Read the excerpt and answer the questions that follow.

IV. Method

The empirical study of legal consciousness presents several methodological challenges. Legal consciousness is complex and difficult to inquire about without inventing it for the subjects, or, at the very least, biasing the subjects' responses. Only through in-depth interviews can legal consciousness emerge, leaving the researcher with lengthy transcripts and the daunting task of using them to determine how to gauge variation in legal consciousness and how this relates to broader social structures.

Early studies attempted to capture the complexities of legal consciousness through observation and in-depth interviews with small samples (see Ewick and Silbey 1992; White 1991; Merry 1990; Sarat 1990). These methods were necessary as theories of legal consciousness were developing. More recently, scholars of legal consciousness have begun to advocate broader data collection to understand variation in legal consciousness and to map the relationship between consciousness and social structure (McCann 1999; Ewick & Silbey 1998; McCann & March 1996). In contrast, studies of political tolerance have surveyed large, randomly selected samples of citizens. The structured protocols of this line of research document attitudes and opinions, but do not allow for an in-depth understanding of legal consciousness.

I bridge this gap by using qualitative research techniques to probe the complexity of legal consciousness, while also interviewing a large enough number of subjects of different races, genders, and classes $(n = 100)$ to begin to gauge variation in it. The combination of field observation and in-depth interviews proved especially valuable. The field observations allowed me to witness and record various types of interactions between strangers in public places. Because I observed many subjects being harassed in public and their reactions to such comments, I was able to guard against the tendency some subjects might have had to inflate

(Continued)

---

[1] Laura Beth Nielsen, "Situating Legal Consciousness: Experiences and Attitudes of Ordinary Citizens about Law and Street Harassment," *Law and Society Review* 34, no. 4 (2000): 1055–90. Reprinted with permission of John Wiley & Sons, Inc.

(Continued)

the bravado with which they responded to such comments. Of course, simply observing was not sufficient because I needed to learn how the subjects *experienced* such interactions, not simply how they responded. The in-depth interviews provided an opportunity to gain an understanding of how individuals think about such interactions, resulting in a "mutuality" between participant observation and in-depth interviews (Lofland & Lofland 1995).

I systematically sampled subjects from the public places I observed. This strategy has several advantages. First, I knew that the subjects were consumers of public space, and thus they constituted a set of potential targets for offensive public speech. From my observations at different locations at different times, I also had some appreciation for what the subjects experienced. Second, by approaching subjects in person, I could establish rapport in a way that would have been impossible if I had initiated contact by telephone. This rapport was essential, given the sensitive nature of the interview questions. Asking subjects about experiences with offensive racist and sexist speech required speaking bluntly and using racial epithets as examples. It would have been difficult to gain consent without such personal contact.

I followed systematic procedures to construct a sample that, while not a probability sample, included different types of people and minimized the possibility of researcher-biased selections because of my personal prepossessions and characteristics. Of course, my presence in the public spaces might have altered the nature of the interactions that took place. Yet in most instances I was simply another person in the crowd and did not have much impact on the obvious interactions taking place.

I conducted a detailed assessment of data sites with the objective of maximizing variation in the socioeconomic status of potential subjects and guarding against idiosyncratic factors that might bias the results (Lofland & Lofland 1995). First, I selected field sites in a variety of locations in three communities in the San Francisco, California, Bay Area (Orinda, Berkeley/Oakland, and San Francisco) to insure broad representation across race, socioeconomic status, and gender among subjects selected to participate in the interviews. Second, I varied the day of the week, going to each of the locations on weekdays and weekends. Third, I varied the time of day by observing in each location during day, evening, and night hours. The field sites I selected were public places, such as sidewalks, public transportation terminals, and bus stops. Finally, to guard against approaching only potential subjects with whom I felt comfortable and to randomize subject selection within field sites, I devised a system whereby each person in the site had an equal chance of being approached.[8] I selected individuals to approach and asked whether they would participate in an interview about interactions among strangers in public places. I continued such selections until I achieved numerical goals for respondents with certain racial and gender characteristics. I oversampled white women and people of color for analytic purposes. Thus, even though I randomized selections within demographic subgroups and within strategically selected locations, this was not a random sample.[9]

---

[8] When I entered a field site, I recorded the scene in my field notes, noting the date, time of day, location, and characteristics of the people occupying that location. I also noted all instances of street harassment. I observed interactions, noting the types of individuals who made comments to strangers, and what responses they received. To determine whom to approach, I randomly selected a side of the location (north or south, east or west) by the flip of a coin. I rolled a die to determine the interval among individuals I would approach; for example, if the coin came up "heads" I went to the north side of the location (such as a train platform); then, if the die came up "3," I approached every third person to ask if he or she would be willing to participate.

[9] In the analyses that follow, I emphasize comparisons across race and gender and limit the statistical analysis to simple chi-square tests for differences across groups. Given the size of the sample, the results should be seen as suggestive in a statistical sense and worthy of examination in larger sample designs.

a. What type of sample did the author use?

_____

_____

b. How did she try to limit bias in her sample?

_____

_____

_____

_____

_____

_____

_____

_____

c. How did the author's method of selecting her subjects ensure that they were appropriate for her study?

_____

_____

_____

_____

_____

_____

_____

_____

_____

Exercise 7–4. Consider this hypothesis: High school students have political beliefs and attitudes similar to those of their parents. To test this hypothesis, both students and parents will be sent questionnaires and their responses compared. The work will be done at "South High," which has an enrollment of 2,000. Here are some ideas for collecting the data. In each instance identify the sampling design and indicate whether it would produce data for a satisfactory test of the hypothesis. Briefly explain your answer. To what populations, if any, could the results be generalized? (*Note:* Do not worry about aspects of the project such as how questionnaires will be matched or obtaining permissions from the school board and/or others.)

a. Proposed sampling scheme: The investigator takes the first and last names (and addresses) from every other page of South High's student directory and mails a questionnaire to those students and their parents.

_____

_____

_____

_____

_____

b. Proposed sampling scheme: Beginning March 1 at 3:30, the investigator stands outside the entrance to South High and hands out questionnaires to passing students and asks that they and their parents return them.

_____

_____

_____

_____

_____

c. Proposed sampling scheme: Investigator asks South High's assistant principal to generate a random list of 200 student names and addresses. Each of these students and his or her parents are mailed a questionnaire.

_____

_____

_____

_____

_____

d. Proposed sampling scheme: The investigator asks the guidance counselor for the names of exactly fifty college-prep students, fifty general study students, fifty vocational educational students, and fifty other students of any kind.

_____

_____

_____

_____

_____

e. Proposed sampling scheme: The investigator asks South High's assistant principal to draw (randomly) fifty names from each class (freshman, sophomore, junior, and senior). Each of these students and his or her parents are mailed a questionnaire.

_____

_____

_____

_____

_____

Exercise 7–5. Suppose you work in the governor's office in Maryland. You have been asked to compare the experiences of businesses owned by various ethnic groups with respect to their interaction with the state economic development office. Because all businesses must register with your state, you have a current list of all businesses and their addresses. Unfortunately, your information does not contain data about the ethnicity of the owners. You plan to send a questionnaire to a sample of business owners. Now the question of sample size comes up. Your office has limited funds but needs to make reliable inferences. Fortunately, U.S. Census Bureau data indicate the percentage of firms owned by various ethnic groups, as shown in Table 7–1.

TABLE 7–1
Maryland Firms, by Race, 2013

Maryland Firms, by Race, 2013			Expected Numbers for Samples of	
Group	Population	Percentage	200	1,000
White	361,229	68.4		
Black	101,926	19.3		
American Indian/ Alaska Native	3,169	0.6		
Asian	35,912	6.8		
Hispanic	25,877	4.9		
Total	528,113	100.0		

Source: Adapted from U.S. Census Bureau, *State and County QuickFacts,* April 22, 2015, http://quickfacts.census.gov/qfd/states/24000.html.

a. If you conduct a total simple random sample of 200, what is the expected number of businesses in each ethnic group? Round to the nearest whole number. Write the numbers in the table.

b. What about a sample of 1,000? Enter these expectations in the last column.

c. Do you see any problems with the sample sizes? Explain.

_____

_____

_____

_____

_____

d. Now assume that business registration forms contained information about the ethnicity of the owners. How would you take a probability sample of 200 owners?

_____

_____

_____

_____

_____

Exercise 7–6.   In this exercise you will contemplate case selection in a comparative study research design. Imagine that you are interested in studying the role nongovernmental organizations play in reducing conflict during civil war. You might begin by limiting your scope to intrastate conflict in the late twentieth century. You can find a list of such conflicts at www.globalsecurity.org/military/world/war/20th-century4.htm. You can find similar lists at other Web sites. Unfortunately for humankind, it is a very long list. As you have limited resources (time during a busy semester being the most pressing), you will use a comparative study research design and limit your exploration through case selection. You have decided that based on your schedule you will only have time to compare five cases.

a. Which five conflicts would you choose from the list?

1. _____

2. _____

3. _____

4. _____

5. _____

b. Why did you choose these five cases? Why are these five more important to study than the others on the list? Did you choose cases that were similar or different in some way? Were you concerned about region of the globe or time period? What about the length of the conflicts or the type of conflict (ones based on ethnicity or ideology, for example)? Please explain your rationale for case selection in detail.

_____

_____

_____

_____

_____

_____

_____

_____

_____

_____

_____

HELPFUL HINTS

Understanding Data Files

Neither the textbook nor this workbook offers much instruction in using computer software to analyze data. Many software packages are available, and political scientists have not adopted a standard. Your instructor will guide your use of the program adopted for the course.

Nevertheless, most software works the same way, and we can provide a few general tips that may be helpful for getting data into a program such as SPSS.

File extensions. Information is stored electronically in different formats. You can often tell the format by looking at the file name and especially at the *file extension*, which comprises a period and three letters. Knowing the file format lets you pick the correct program or program options when reading or opening a data file. Some common file extensions are as follows:

■ **.txt** for "text" data or information. A text file contains just alphanumeric characters (for example, letters, digits, punctuation marks, a few symbols) and, when printed, looks just like something created on a typewriter or simple printer. If a program "thinks" it's reading text data, it won't recognize hidden codes for different fonts, graphics, and so forth. Consequently, if your word processor

(Continued)

(Continued)

or editor (for example, NotePad) shows you a lot of gibberish, chances are that the file is not simple text. When you double-click a file name of this sort, your operating system's default word processor or editor will automatically try to open it. An example of a text file is "anes2004readme.txt," which describes a set of data pertaining to the 2004 American national election.

■ **.dat** for "data." The extension does indeed suggest data, but files of this type sometimes contain alphanumeric characters as well. In either case they can be loaded into a word processor. Moreover, some statistical programs recognize the ".dat" extension as data and will try to open the data. SPSS, for example, reads these files. Go to "File" and then "Read Text Data." After locating the file in the menu box, the program will start a Text Import Wizard, which takes you step by step through getting the data. Examples of this format are "randomnumbers.dat," "surveytext.dat," and "surveydigits.dat." Depending on your system's configuration, double-clicking on ".dat" extension names will start a word processor or possibly a statistical program. But you can first run the program you want and then read the file.

■ **.doc** for "document" information. This extension usually means Microsoft Word–formatted information that contains hidden formatting codes and so forth. Unless you have changed options on your computer or do not have the Windows operating system, double-clicking a ".doc" file will start Microsoft Word. (As we mention in the following text, other word processors can open some versions of Word files, so you are not limited to just that package.)

■ **.sav** and **.por** for SPSS data files. These file extensions "belong" to SPSS. Like most statistical software programs, SPSS allows you to give descriptive names to variables and their individual values and to create new variables or transform and recode variables in all sorts of ways. All this auxiliary information, along with the raw data, can then be saved in one file so that it is available for reuse at a later time. The file extension ".sav" stands for "saved." SPSS data dictionary information can be saved in a slightly more general format called ".por" for "portable." (We frequently use this option.) These files can be read by SPSS running on operating systems like Unix. An example is "survey-digits.por."

File structure and size. The file structure we use is quite simple: data are presented and stored in rectangular arrays in which each row represents a case (an individual, for instance), and the columns contain values of the variables. So if a file has 1,000 cases and two variables, the data structure is a 1,000-by-2 rectangular array of cells. Each cell holds a value for a specific case for a specific variable. (To save space on the printed page, we sometimes use "unstacked" columns.) The "surveydigits.dat" file, for example, has five columns of identification numbers and five columns of responses to make a 1,000-by-10-column matrix. But we arranged the numbers this way purely for convenience. Most software lets you stack columns on top of one another. Therefore, if you wanted, you could stack the columns 1, 3, 5, 7, and 9 of "surveydigits.dat" on top of each other and do the same with columns 2, 4, 6, 8, 10, to make a 5,000-by-2 array. Also notice that files with more than, say, thirty variables need more than one line when shown on a monitor or printed on an average piece of paper. For these data sets the lines will "wrap" around, making them difficult to read. Finally, if you are thinking about copying a file, you can roughly estimate the file's size by multiplying the number of variables by the number of cases.

File delimiters. Most of the time the data points are separated by simple blank spaces. Occasionally, however, data are separated by tabs. (In many systems the tab character is denoted by "^t"—that is, a caret and lowercase *t*.) Sometimes you have to keep this in mind when using certain software, but many times a program will detect the tabs automatically.

Case ID numbers. Some data files have explicit identification numbers for each case (for example, "surveytext.dat" and "survey digits.dat"). In others the case number is just the row number. When you view the data matrix in a program, you will be able to determine which is the case.

Note: Our Web site (http://edge.sagepub.com/johnson8e) contains all the data files.

Exercise 7–7.   Imagine that you are working on a research project at your school on student attitudes. You are interested in measuring how responsive administrators are to issues raised by the student body through its student government using a probability sample. Assuming that your population of interest includes every enrolled student at the school, how might you build a sampling frame *without asking for or using a complete list of enrolled students?* In answering this question, think about the information that is publicly available to you and about different methods of drawing a sample.

a.   How would you build your sampling frame?

_____

_____

_____

_____

_____

_____

b.   Consider the challenges you may face in the plan you described in part a. Will your sampling frame duplicate the population of interest? Are there portions of the population that may not be included in the sampling frame?

_____

_____

_____

_____

c.   Why is it problematic if the sampling frame is different from the population of interest?

_____

_____

_____

Exercise 7–8. Read the following abstract from a project called "Black Oversample for the American National Election Study," by Tasha Philpot and Daron Shaw, then answer the questions below.[2]

Blacks have been somewhat relegated to the sidelines in recent years by scholars more interested in America's burgeoning Latino and Asian populations. Setting aside the unique experience and place of blacks in American history and consciousness, this is regrettable for two reasons. First, the black population is often written off as "monolithic." This has, in our view, never been true but it is an increasingly troubling myth given the growing diversity of the black population. Second, many of the political and social events of the past decade have been particularly relevant for blacks: the 2000 election controversy, redistricting after the 2000 Census, and the devastation and revelations of Hurricane Katrina. If scholars are to usefully inform the public debate on matters such as mass opinion, representation, and the role of race in politics, we need a comprehensive and reliable source of data. A black over-sample within the context of the traditional ANES is an extremely effective way to achieve this.

Although the ANES has been the dominant source of data for the classic studies of turnout, partisanship, ideology, congressional voting, and political sophistication, it has been of limited use for the study of black opinion and behavior. Our study allows scholars to examine black opinion across the wide and disparate range of the ANES core instrument, as well as yielding insight into issues that predominantly concern African Americans. Furthermore, a black over-sample facilitates attitudinal and behavioral comparisons with other racial and ethnic groups as never before.

Our approach is straight-forward: working in cooperation with the ANES team at Michigan, we have over-seen the recruitment, interviewing, and data collection for an over-sample of African Americans. Based on the current specifications for the 2008 ANES pre- and post-election sample, approximately 290 black respondents are interviewed, making stand-alone analyses of black opinion, attitudes, and behavior problematic. Our study adds another 310 black respondents and uses the expanded number of primary sampling units (PSU) to obtain a larger, more representative black sub-sample. In addition, by adding 10 PSUs we are able to increase the number of black respondents from racially mixed—as opposed to predominantly black—neighborhoods.

This 2008 ANES black over-sample constitutes a substantial "public good": it significantly enhances our ability to gauge the range, diversity, and determinants of African-American political opinion and vote choice. Furthermore, it facilitates informed comparisons to whites and Latinos at a time when such comparisons are especially useful to our conceptions of politics and representation.

a. Why is this "over-sample" an example of the disproportionate sampling method?

_____

_____

b. Why is a disproportionate sample like this better than a simple random sample?

_____

_____

c. Why do the authors refer to this disproportionate sample as a "public good?"

_____

_____

_____

---

[2] Tasha Philpot and Daron Shaw, Black Oversample for the American National Election Study," *Grantome*, http://grantome.com/grant/ NSF/SES-0752987. Reprinted by permission of the authors.

Exercise 7–9. You are working for a nonprofit agency based in New York that is trying to encourage political mobilization in South Africa. The organization plans to interview South Africans about attitudes toward participation and elections before developing a plan of action. In the space below discuss the advantages and disadvantages of using a cluster sample.

_____

_____

_____

_____

_____

_____

_____

_____

_____

_____

CHAPTER 8

Making Empirical Observations

Firsthand Observation

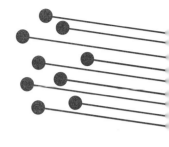

Observation of political activities and behaviors is a data collection method that can be used profitably by political scientists. Although some observation studies require a considerable amount of time and a researcher's presence in a particular location, most of us are likely to have used this method to learn about politics in a casual manner, without traveling great distances or staying in a setting for a long time. With some imagination, you can find numerous opportunities to use observation systematically to collect information about political phenomena. For example, you can judge community concern about proposed school budgets by attending school board meetings. You can observe the nature of political comments made by those around you and how others react. You can assess power relationships or leadership styles by observing physical and verbal cues given by participants in various settings.

Exercise 8-1.   David A. Bositis notes in his article, "Some Observations on the Participant Method," *Political Behavior* 10 (Winter 1988): 333–48, that "a key feature of participant observation design is an ability to both observe behavior and to provoke behaviors to be subsequently observed." Read Bositis's article and think of situations in which your participation (either your physical presence or verbal communication) could provoke behaviors to be observed. Are any ethical considerations raised by these situations? If not, think of a situation that poses some ethical issues. If all of the situations you thought of pose ethical issues, try to think of one that does not raise ethical issues.

_____

_____

_____

_____

_____

_____

_____

_____

Exercise 8–2.   Read Laura Beth Nielsen's article, "Situating Legal Consciousness: Experiences and Attitudes of Ordinary Citizens about Law and Street Harassment," *Law and Society Review* 34, no. 4 (2000): 1055–90, especially the "Method" section beginning on page 1061. (You can find the excerpt in this workbook in chapter 7, exercise 7–3.) How did observation play a role in her research?

_____

_____

_____

_____

_____

_____

_____

_____

Exercise 8–3.   Read James M. Glaser's article, "The Challenges of Campaign Watching: Seven Lessons of Participant-Observation Research," *PS: Political Science and Politics* 29 (September 1996): 533–37. (The article is available from JSTOR.) Why is participant observation important to studying political campaigns? How important is flexibility in this type of research?

_____

_____

_____

_____

_____

Exercise 8–4.   This exercise will allow you to put your participant observation skills to the test by attending a local political meeting, such as a city council meeting or a town hall meeting. First, develop a hypothesis about the behavior you will witness. You might want to think about how elected officials will interact with each other or how citizens attending the meeting will behave. Or, you might have ideas about the kinds of issues citizens will discuss, such as local ordinances, requests for services, or complaints about a problem in the community. You can hypothesize just about anything that is appropriate for the meeting you choose.

a.   Write your hypothesis on the line below.

_____

b.   Which political meeting did you attend?

_____

c. After attending the meeting, what observations did you make that contributed to testing your hypothesis?

_____

_____

_____

_____

_____

d. Based on your observations, was your hypothesis correct? Why or why not?

_____

_____

_____

_____

HELPFUL HINTS

Be Careful When Observing the Public

In chapter 8 we discuss several ways to make direct and indirect observations. In general, and especially if you are working through a university or college, you must obtain the informed consent of individuals you question in a poll or survey or use in an experiment. Getting this agreement may be a straightforward matter of asking for permission, which subjects should feel completely free to give or deny. You may, however, be involved in direct or indirect observation of people (or their possessions) that does not involve face-to-face contact. (Suppose, for example, you want to observe a protest march.) Even in this case you should accept some standards of responsible and courteous research:

■ Be aware of your personal safety. Make sure someone knows where you are going. Carry proper identification. It also wouldn't hurt to carry a letter of introduction from your professor, supervisor, or employer.

■ Depending on the nature of the study, it may be wise to contact local authorities to tell them that you will be in a certain area collecting data in a particular way. If you seem to be just hanging around a neighborhood, park, or schoolyard, you could possibly be reported as someone acting suspicious.

■ Always ask permission if you enter private property. If no one is available to give permission, come back later or try somewhere else. Even in many public accommodations, such as arenas or department stores, you will probably need to get prior approval to do your research.

■ Respect people's privacy even when they are in public places.

■ Do not misrepresent yourself. Some of our students once had an issue with this. They wanted to compare the treatment that whites and nonwhites received in rural welfare offices. They pretended to be needy and applied for public assistance in order to observe the behavior of welfare officers. By doing this, however, they were breaking state and federal laws. They got off with a warning, but it's always a big mistake to fake being someone you're not just to collect data.

■ Be willing, even eager, to share your results with those who have asked about your activities. Volunteer to send them a copy of your study. (Doing so will encourage cooperation.)

■ When observing a demonstration, protest march, debate, or similar confrontation, do not appear to take sides.

Exercise 8–5. Some direct observation research takes place in a laboratory where researchers can carefully control conditions, such as the number of participants, the physical environment, stimuli, etc. Other observation takes place in a natural setting where researchers have no control but can observe real interactions. Sometimes observation is used to test hypotheses, and in other cases observation is used to generate hypotheses. In this exercise you will make observations in a natural setting using streaming video of a U.S. Senate committee hearing. Your task is to develop hypotheses about how elected officials interact with witnesses. Although the hearing is from long ago (1969!), you should find the interaction between the witness and the senator engaging to watch.

a. Watch the six-minute excerpt of the Senate Committee on Commerce hearing on the Public Broadcasting Act of 1967 at www.americanrhetoric.com/speeches/fredrogerssenatetestimonypbs.htm. List your observations on the interaction between Senator Pastore and the witness, Fred Rogers. These observations might be about speaking tone, number of interruptions, speech content, or many other concepts related to the interaction between political actors. You may find the transcript of the video clip useful in making observations as well.[1]

b. Record your observations in the space below.

_____

_____

_____

_____

_____

_____

_____

_____

_____

c. List three hypotheses you could test about the interaction between elected officials and witnesses based on your observations.

1. _____

2. _____

3. _____

---

[1] Extension of Authorizations under the Public Broadcasting Act of 1967, Hearings, 91st Cong., 1st sess., on S. 1242, April 30 and May 1, 1969, Washington, U.S. Government Printing Office, 1969; Y 4.C 73/2: 91-5.

Exercise 8–6. Imagine that you are interested in studying how people collect and use political information when making a decision. You are particularly interested in how much information people feel they need to make an informed decision. You want to test the hypothesis that people will seek to collect more information before making a decision when it is easy to collect information. For this exercise assume that you have access to a suitable laboratory space with top-of-the-line audio-video equipment for recording behavior and a representative sample of willing participants. You can also feel free to spend a great deal of virtual money to create the ultimate observational design. (*Hint:* You should begin by identifying the decision that participants must make. Remember also that you will need to assess how people make use of easy-to-find information and hard-to-find information. How can you make information easy or hard to find?)

a. In the space below, describe how you could use a laboratory setting to test this hypothesis through direct observation.

_____

_____

_____

_____

_____

_____

_____

_____

_____

b. In the space below, explain why you chose to design your observational study in this way. Why might observation in a laboratory be better than in a natural setting to test a hypothesis like this?

_____

_____

_____

Exercise 8–7. The goal of ethnography is to make cultural interpretations through personal observation of everyday life. In order to make these interpretations, researchers immerse themselves in the community under study. As a student you are in a position to make direct observations of political life on campus. In this exercise you will make direct observations of how the campus community embraces recycling efforts. Most colleges and universities have recycling programs in place and encourage members of the campus community to recycle. For this exercise you should find a spot in a cafeteria at your school where you can observe a garbage bin and a recycling bin in near proximity—ideally next to each other. For a short period (twenty to thirty minutes) during a busy time in the cafeteria, such as lunch or dinner, make observations about how members of the campus community embrace recycling. Do people recycle? Are they using each bin as intended? Do some people carefully divide trays into multiple bins? Do some people remind their friends to recycle? Are there recycling instructions posted near the bin? Are there recycling instructions posted elsewhere in the building?

a. Make your observations on the lines below. Indicate when, where, and for how long you made these observations.

_____

_____

_____

_____

_____

_____

_____

_____

_____

_____

b. What interpretations can you make about the recycling movement at your school based on these observations?

_____

_____

_____

_____

c. How might you gain a better understanding of recycling as a social norm of behavior at your school? What other kinds of observations might be necessary?

_____

_____

_____

_____

CHAPTER 9

Document Analysis
Using the Written Record

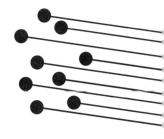

In chapter 9 we discuss using the record-keeping activities of institutions, organizations, and individuals as sources of data for research projects. In some situations, as with the *Statistical Abstract of the United States* or the World Bank's *World Development Indicators,* the records provide data that are directly usable as operational measures of concepts and variables, although you will need to decide how well these data measure the concepts you want to measure. In other cases, to create measures of your variables you will need to analyze the records using, for example, content analysis. Much of the data you collect will be part of the "running" record—that is, collected on a routine basis by public organizations such as the U.S. Census Bureau. It is less likely that you will use "episodic" records, which are those records that are preserved in a casual, personal, and accidental manner.

Exercise 9–1. American presidents deliver at least one State of the Union address per year. Today the speech takes place in the U.S. House of Representatives in front of most of the nation's representatives, senators, Supreme Court justices, Cabinet officials, Joint Chiefs of Staff, and other national political figures. This was not always the case. In fact, there is a good bit of variability in how the address is delivered, its length, its content, and who attends. In the questions below you will rely on content analysis data archived by the American Presidency Project, available at www.presidency.ucsb.edu/sou.php.

a. Use data about the length of the State of the Union address to generate a hypothesis about the relationship between address type (written or spoken) and address length, measured in words. You will find the data at www.presidency.ucsb.edu/sou_words.php.

b. Presidents often invite special guests to the State of the Union address and acknowledge those guests during the address. Use data about the guests sitting in the House Gallery during the State of the Union address to generate a hypothesis about the number of these guests. You will find the data at www.presidency.ucsb.edu/sou_gallery.php.

c. Write a hypothesis about the proportion of male to female guests sitting in the House Gallery. For this hypothesis you will need to use your best judgment based on the listed names. You will find the data at www.presidency.ucsb.edu/sou_gallery.php.

d. Explain why coding gender based on name alone might cause problems in making inferences if your gender count data were used in a real content analysis project.

_____

_____

_____

_____

Exercise 9–2. In this exercise you will perform a simplified content analysis. Scholarly content analyses typically include many individual documents or other sources of data. For this exercise you will try your hand at analyzing the content of just one document. In this hypothetical project, you are interested in learning about the balance between issue content and content about a party's candidates. To begin, read the following Whig Party political platform from 1844.

> Resolved, That, in presenting to the country the names of Henry Clay for president, and of Theodore Frelinghuysen for vice-president of the United States, this Convention is actuated by the conviction that all the great principles of the Whig party—principles inseparable from the public honor and prosperity—will be maintained and advanced by these candidates.
>
> Resolved, That these principles may be summed as comprising, a well-regulated currency; a tariff for revenue to defray the necessary expenses of the government, and discriminating with special reference to the protection of the domestic labor of the country; the distribution of the proceeds of the sales of the public lands; a single term for the presidency; a reform of executive usurpations;—and, generally—such an administration of the affairs of the country as shall impart to every branch of the public service the greatest practicable efficiency, controlled by a well regulated and wise economy.
>
> Resolved, That the name of Henry Clay needs no eulogy; the history of the country since his first appearance in public life is his history; its brightest pages of prosperity and success are identified with the principles which he has upheld, as its darkest and more disastrous pages are with every material departure in our public policy from those principles.
>
> Resolved, That in Theodore Frelinghuysen we present a man pledged alike by his revolutionary ancestry and his own public course to every measure calculated to sustain the honor and interest of the country. Inheriting the principles as well as the name of a father who, with Washington, on the fields of Trenton and of Monmouth, perilled life in the contest for liberty, and afterwards, as a senator of the United States, acted with Washington in establishing and perpetuating that liberty, Theodore Frelinghuysen, by his course as Attorney-General of the State of New Jersey for twelve years, and subsequently as a senator of the United States for several years, was always strenuous on the side of law, order, and the constitution, while as a private man, his head, his hand, and his heart have been given without stint to the cause of morals, education, philanthropy, and religion.[1]

a. How would you propose measuring the amount of the platform dedicated to the Whig Party's issue positions and the amount dedicated to the party's presidential candidate, Henry Clay? Would your recording unit be the number of words, number of sentences, number of paragraphs, or another metric? Explain why below.

_____

_____

_____

_____

---

[1] "Political Party Platforms: Whig Party Platform of 1844," May 1, 1844, *American Presidency Project*, www.presidency.ucsb.edu/ws/index.php?pid=25852.

b. Remember that you are interested in the balance between issue content and candidate content in platforms. This platform, and most others, includes other information as well. Do you think it would be better to record the proportion of issue content to candidate content (62 percent issue to 38 percent candidate, for example) or to record the percentage of the overall platform that each component represents (53 percent issue, 14 percent candidate, 33 percent other, for example). What are the relative advantages of each strategy?

_____

_____

_____

_____

c. Because this platform is from 1844, there may be words you do not recognize and words that may have changed meaning over time. For example, the word _egregious_ once meant "standing out from the flock," but now it has a negative connotation. If you were to undertake a content analysis of historical documents, how might you tackle the problem of what words meant at the time they were used?

_____

_____

_____

_____

d. To complicate matters, let us assume that you want to code the tone of language used to describe candidates. How might you think about coding tone? Give some examples from the words and phrases used in the platform.

_____

_____

_____

_____

Exercise 9–3.   In this exercise you will perform a simplified content analysis. Scholarly content analyses typically include many individual documents or other sources of data. You will try your hand at analyzing the content of just one video clip. Content analysis often involves identifying whether important characteristics are present or absent in a document or other form of content. In this exercise you will create a content analysis coding scheme for presidential campaign advertisements. In a real content analysis, you might use your coding scheme to code the content of dozens or hundreds of advertisements from one or more candidate in one or more elections. Here you will use your coding scheme to code just one campaign commercial. This exercise is intended to help you understand how a coding scheme is used in a content analysis and make you aware of the difficulties researchers face in creating a coding scheme and coding content.

a. Your first task is to list five important characteristics about campaign commercials on the lines below. You might consider a number of characteristics, such as the type of commercial (issue oriented, biographical, attack, or negative); the use of sound or music; whether the candidate or the opposition physically appears in the ad; or even the use of footnotes for claims.

_____

_____

b. Explain how you could measure the presence of each of the characteristics you identified in part a. For example, consider the characteristic, "Candidate spoke in ad." You could watch an ad and record a "1" on a spreadsheet if the candidate spoke in the ad or a "0" if the candidate did not.

_____

_____

_____

_____

_____

c. Using the Obama ad, "This Is a Clear Choice," from the 2012 presidential election, apply your coding scheme and record the results below. You can find the ad clip at www.livingroomcandidate.org/commercials/2012. You might also find this transcript useful:

Clinton: This election, to me, is about which candidate is more likely to return us to full employment. This is a clear choice. The Republican plan is to cut more taxes on upper-income people and go back to deregulation. That's what got us in trouble in the first place. President Obama has a plan to rebuild America from the ground up. Investing in innovation, education, and job training. It only works if there is a strong middle class. That's what happened when I was president. We need to keep going with his plan.

Obama: I'm Barack Obama and I approve this message.

_____

_____

_____

d. Having used your coding scheme just once, reflect on how you might improve it if you were to apply it to hundreds of ads. How would you improve your coding scheme? Why would you make these changes?

_____

_____

_____

_____

_____

Example 9–4. For this exercise you will consider how you might use the running record to explore ideas about public policy. Imagine that you are interested in writing a research paper on climate change in Western Europe. Table 9–1 includes data from the United Nations on carbon dioxide emissions in fifteen Western European countries.

a. Complete the rest of the table by finding the population for each country. Note that population would be best measured in 2012, but 2011 or 2010 will work as well. Also, make sure to label the unit in parentheses at the top of the column (thousands, millions, etc.) and include the citation for where you found the data here: _____

b. How might you use this data to test ideas about climate change? On the line below generate a hypothesis about climate change using the data in table 9–1.

_____

c. What additional data would you want to collect from the running record to test more ideas about climate change? Explore the datasets available from the United Nations at http://data.un.org/DataMartInfo.aspx or search for United Nations data using a Web browser. List four variables or data sets you would find useful and explain why.

_____

_____

TABLE 9–1

Western European Carbon Dioxide Emissions, 2012

Country	CO2 Emissions, Gigatons	Population ( )
Austria	67,733	
Belgium	100,659	
Denmark	40,799	
France	368,845	
Germany	821,718	
Ireland	38,011	
Italy	386,667	
Liechtenstein	189	
Luxembourg	10,870	
Monaco	83	
Netherlands	165,262	
Portugal	50,310	
Spain	276,637	
Switzerland	43,251	
United Kingdom	483,424	

Source: "Carbon Dioxide (CO2) Emissions without Land Use, Land-Use Change and Forestry (LULUCF), in Gigagrams (Gg)," *UN Data*, 2015, http://data.un.org/Data.aspx?d= GHG&f=seriesID%3aCO2.

_____

_____

_____

_____

_____

_____

_____

Exercise 9–5.   Imagine that you are interested in how newspapers cover nuclear proliferation. You decide to use secondhand data from the running record rather than collecting the data yourself due to resource limitations. The Policy Agendas Project, as described in more length in the text, includes data on issue content for a random sample of entries in the *New York Times* index since 1964. The index includes thousands of entries per year and includes a short summary of each story, along with information about where in the newspaper each story appeared and its length.

a.   Identify and explain potential problems you may encounter by relying on a random sample of *New York Times* news items rather than all of the stories in each day's newspaper if you are interested in a single issue, such as nuclear proliferation. Is there any advantage to having data on all of the stories?

_____

_____

_____

Read the passage below from the Policy Agendas Project *New York Times* codebook (emphases added):

There are *two complications* to the *New York Times* and its Index that users should keep in mind. First is that occasional format changes have led to *different numbers of articles on each page*. Second is that the *New York Times* and its Index have *varied in size over the decades*. An accompanying dataset, *New York Times* Index Weights (available on our website), gives detailed information on the *number of pages in the Index* and on an estimate of the *number of articles per page* for each of the years included in our dataset.[2]

b.   How would the first complication, different numbers of articles on each page in the newspaper, affect an analysis of front-page stories on nuclear proliferation?

_____

_____

_____

_____

[2] "New York Times Index Data Codebook," *Policy Agendas Project 2014*, www.policyagendas.org.

c. How would the second complication, varying numbers of pages in the index, affect an analysis of news content?

_____

_____

Exercise 9-6. The Pew Research Center performs many content analyses. It has established a protocol it follows when coding content that relies on highly trained employees following a set of written rules. For example, when coding whether content is either supportive or opposing in regard to a particular issue of interest, Pew might require that each supportive or opposing comment be tallied and that the total number of supportive statements must be at least twice the total number of opposing comments for the content to be labeled as supportive overall, or vice versa. Pew also states that

> in order to ensure reliability and consistency, we perform intercoder tests for all coders involved in a project. To do this, we choose a random selection of stories from the overall sample (usually 5%-7%) and have each person code them independently. We then compare the results to get the rates of agreement for all variables. The center follows rigorous academic standards, and we only publish variables where we have rates of agreement of 80% or higher (in most cases, much higher). If we test variables and find rates of less than 80%, we continue training, clarifying rules and/or revising the variable until we reach that level in subsequent tests.[3]

a. What does Pew mean by _reliability_ and _consistency_ in this passage? Why are these important concepts in a content analysis?

_____

_____

_____

b. Do you feel that an 80 percent rate of agreement is high enough to assure that coders are labeling material in a consistent and similar manner?

_____

_____

_____

Pew also uses computers to code content for analysis. While the main advantages of using computers are the greatly increased speed with which material can be coded and the reliability—a computer will code material the same way every time when following an algorithm—Pew notes the following disadvantages:

> [C]omputer coding has some built-in disadvantages as well. First, it can only work on text that has been digitized (i.e., in the form of a website story) and is publicly available, so certain channels of media are difficult to reliably code, including local television and radio. Second, it remains limited in its ability to judge the kind of nuance that seems relatively straightforward to the human coder: Is this article generally favorable toward the president, or generally unfavorable? Is the writer using sarcasm, or is the writer

---

[3] You can read this excerpt and more about Pew's content analysis methodology at "Human Coding of News Media," _Pew Research Center_, http://www.pewresearch.org/methodology/about-content-analysis/human-coding-of-news-media/.

being serious? Computer algorithms that do this kind of "sentiment analysis" are being created, but to some extent these remain early days. Third, it can sometimes be difficult to understand the shape and limits of the universe of digitized data that is being coded, the days of the discrete, delimited newsprint paper being today behind us.[4]

c. Consider the three disadvantages Pew lists. Which do you think is the most important limitation to using computers for content analysis. Why? Explain your answer below.

_____

_____

_____

_____

[4] "Computer Coding," *Pew Research Center*, http://www.pewresearch.org/methodology/about-content-analysis/computer-coding/.

CHAPTER 10

Survey Research and Interviewing

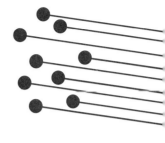

The use of survey research and elite interviewing has become far more than a staple of empirical political science. These tools now guide decision makers' thinking about public policy, appear as data in support of partisan arguments, and offer the mass media a way to inform consumers about what is going on in the world. The reason is obvious: interviewing and polling supposedly provide objective "scientific" data. If, for example, a politician or an organization can claim that more than half of the public favors a particular position, that stance might acquire a legitimacy it would not otherwise enjoy. Polls and surveys are so frequently used to acquire information about what people think that they have become a part of the everyday parlance of even apolitical citizens.

As common and impressive as these methods are, however, they need to be considered carefully. After all, everyone knows the adage, "Ask a dumb question, get a dumb answer." It behooves students of politics to become familiar with what these research techniques can and cannot accomplish.

Just as they do in the natural sciences, measuring and recording devices in the social sciences rest on theories. In surveying and elite interviewing, the most fundamental premises are that respondents have certain information sought by the investigator, that the respondents know how and are willing to provide this information, and, perhaps most importantly, that everyone involved in the process shares to a high degree of approximation the meanings of the words and symbols employed in the information exchange. That is why chapter 10 stresses the importance of thinking carefully about how questions are worded and presented to respondents, who may or may not care much about the researcher's topic. We note in particular that if questions are ambiguous or threatening, people may not answer them or not answer them truthfully.

Please take some time to consider the assignments. They demand not only that you understand specific terms (*open-ended*, for example) but also that you fully grasp the difficulty of designing an effective questionnaire, whether it is intended for an elite or a mass audience.

Exercise 10–1. Suppose you are thinking of surveying the general public about party identification, the psychological feeling of closeness or attachment to a political party. (Party identification is *not* party registration, which is a formal designation. It is an attitude or disposition toward a party.)

a. Write an example of a closed-ended question. Make sure that the possible answers to the question are both exclusive and exhaustive.

_____

_____

_____

_____

b. Write an example of an open-ended question.

_____

_____

_____

_____

c. Write an example of a leading question that would likely yield more Republican respondents.

_____

_____

_____

_____

Exercise 10–2.   For each of the concepts or topics listed below, which would be most appropriate to use to gather information, a closed- or an open-ended question? Why? If either would be appropriate or possible, explain in sufficient detail to demonstrate your knowledge of the difference between the types of questions.

a. Whether or not a person has lived in a congressional district for more than two years

_____

_____

_____

_____

b. Actions respondent is willing to take to improve community engagement

_____

_____

_____

_____

c. A person's support for or opposition to reestablishing Section 4 of the Voting Rights Act

_____

_____

_____

_____

d. A person's satisfaction with the current Congress's performance

_____

_____

_____

_____

e. How many hours a week a person works

_____

_____

_____

_____

f. What a person knows about the World Bank

_____

_____

_____

_____

g. A person's rating of Senator Joni Ernst's (IA-R) performance in office

_____

_____

_____

_____

h. Support for restructuring Medicare

_____

_____

_____

_____

Exercise 10–3.   Provide a short evaluation or critique of the following survey questions. If you do not see any problems with a question, just say so.

a.   "What is your opinion of a national flat tax? Do you oppose or favor it, or do you have no opinion?"

_____

_____

_____

_____

b.   "When talking with citizens, we find that most of them oppose increasing the federal tax on gasoline. How about you? Would you favor or oppose an increase in the gasoline tax?"

_____

_____

_____

_____

c.   "Would you favor or oppose the state selling its bonds and securities to private companies if it would raise monies to pay for child health care?"

_____

_____

_____

_____

d.   "Since the September 11, 2001, attacks in New York City and Washington, D.C., there has been a great deal of attention paid to terrorism. Do you support increased spending to protect the nation from terrorism?"

_____

_____

_____

_____

e.   "Have you ever used an illegal drug?"

_____

_____

_____

_____

Exercise 10-4. Sometimes it is difficult to write high-quality survey questions that are both reliable and valid (see chapters 5 and 10). It is particularly important to consider content validity (whether you have fully captured the meaning of a concept with a survey question). In this exercise you are to provide a definition for each of the terms listed, write a survey question for each, and explain how each question captures the full meaning of the term.

a. Employment status

_____

_____

_____

_____

b. Attitude toward female officeholders

_____

_____

_____

_____

c. Level of support for the British prime minister

_____

_____

_____

_____

d. Political ideology

_____

_____

_____

_____

e. Level of participation in politics

_____

_____

_____

_____

Exercise 10–5. The Pew Research Center has administered over 480,000 interviews in ninety-one different countries as of 2015, mostly as part of their Global Attitudes and Religion and Public Life projects. These projects are valuable in part because they ask the same questions of people in different parts of the world across time, allowing researchers to measure differences in attitudes among people from different cultures. Survey questions might be translated into eighty or more languages, which requires a great deal of work. According to Pew:

> Translation is a multi-step process. For questions asked on earlier surveys, the center relies on translations used in previous questionnaires in order to maintain comparability of survey data over time. For new questions, Pew Research staff begin by submitting the questions to professional linguists. The linguists evaluate each question for ease of translation and make recommendations to guide proper translation. New questions, along with the linguists' recommendations, are then submitted to local research organizations, which translate the items into the appropriate language(s). Once translations are complete, they are again reviewed by professional linguists, who provide feedback to the translators. Pew Research Center staff are consulted regarding any serious debates about translation, and the center issues final approval of the translated survey instrument prior to fieldwork.[1]

a. Why does Pew use such a complicated process—involving linguists, local research organizations, and translators—to translate questions? How could the translation process affect survey responses?

_____

_____

_____

b. Why is it important that Pew uses the same translations of questions over time? Why not revise translations when questions are reused?

_____

_____

_____

Pew also notes that

> Pew Research Center staff are responsible for the overall design and execution of each cross-national survey project, including topical focus, questionnaire development, countries to be surveyed and sample design. The center's staff frequently contract with a primary vendor to identify local, reputable research organizations, which are hired to translate questionnaires, administer surveys in the field and process data. Both primary vendors and local research organizations are consulted on matters of sampling, fieldwork logistics and translation. In addition, Pew Research often seeks the advice of subject matter experts and experienced survey researchers regarding the design and content of its cross-national studies.[2]

---

[1] Pew Research Center, "Questionnaire Design and Translation," http://www.pewresearch.org/methodology/international-survey-research/questionnaire-design-and-translation/.

[2] You can read this passage and more about Pew's international survey efforts at http://www.pewresearch.org/methodology/international-survey-research/.

c. Why is it important that Pew consults with local research organizations about sampling and fieldwork in foreign countries?

_____

_____

_____

d. When Pew executes cross-national studies, it aims to complete all survey interviews in a three-to-six-week time period. Why is keeping the time period as short as possible important?

_____

_____

_____

Exercise 10–6.   Consider two different survey questions that measure support for the president:

(Question 1) Do you *approve* or *disapprove* of the way Barack Obama is handling his job as president?
(Question 2) How would you rate the job Barack Obama has been doing as president . . . do you *strongly approve, somewhat approve, somewhat disapprove,* or *strongly disapprove* of the job he's been doing?

In the first question, respondents are offered only two answer choices: "approve" and "disapprove." In the second question, respondents are offered four answer choices: "strongly approve," "somewhat approve," "somewhat disapprove," or "strongly disapprove." When Rasmussen, a polling organization, asked each of these questions to different but similar random samples of 800 likely voters in November 2009[3], the results were (with the answer choices for question 2 collapsed into "approve" and "disapprove" for comparison's sake):

(Question 1)   50 percent "approve," 46 percent "disapprove," and 4 percent "don't know"
(Question 2)   47 percent "approve," 52 percent "disapprove," and 1 percent "don't know"

a. Both random samples were similar, so why were the results different? In the space below, explain why you think the inclusion of the "somewhat" categories could have affected the results.

_____

_____

_____

_____

_____

---

[3] Mark Blumenthal, "Why Is Rasmussen So Different?," *Pollster.com*, December 1, 2009, www.pollster.com/blogs/why_is_rasmussen_so_different.html.

b. How does this example help us better understand the importance of question wording?

_____

_____

_____

_____

Exercise 10-7.   Imagine that you are a student who is bored with an assignment on survey question writing. The assignment asks you to write a series of five questions you would ask of voters in a presidential election. To make things more interesting, you decide to write five questions that break all of the rules of question writing. In the space provided write five bad survey questions and explain why they break the rules.

1. _____

_____

_____

_____

2. _____

_____

_____

_____

3. _____

_____

_____

_____

4. _____

_____

_____

_____

5. _____

_____

_____

_____

CHAPTER 11

Making Sense of Data

First Steps

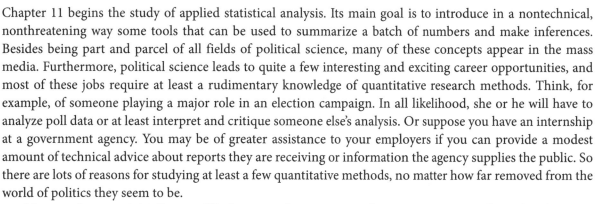

Chapter 11 begins the study of applied statistical analysis. Its main goal is to introduce in a nontechnical, nonthreatening way some tools that can be used to summarize a batch of numbers and make inferences. Besides being part and parcel of all fields of political science, many of these concepts appear in the mass media. Furthermore, political science leads to quite a few interesting and exciting career opportunities, and most of these jobs require at least a rudimentary knowledge of quantitative research methods. Think, for example, of someone playing a major role in an election campaign. In all likelihood, she or he will have to analyze poll data or at least interpret and critique someone else's analysis. Or suppose you have an internship at a government agency. You may be of greater assistance to your employers if you can provide a modest amount of technical advice about reports they are receiving or information the agency supplies the public. So there are lots of reasons for studying at least a few quantitative methods, no matter how far removed from the world of politics they seem to be.

Many students are initially put off by having to learn statistics, but our experience tells us that this aversion often results from unfamiliarity with the subject, not its inherent difficulty. So even if you are one who says, "I stink at math," at least attempt to keep an open mind. We think you may find that these concerns are misplaced.

Here are a few tips:

- **Keep up.** Unlike some subjects that may seem to lend themselves to cramming, statistics is best learned step by step; you should make sure you understand each concept reasonably well before moving on to the next one. And since the ideas are possibly daunting at first sight, it is easy to get lost if you try to learn everything all at once. This is, in short, one course where it pays to stay on top of the readings and assignments.

- **Learn by doing**. You can't get into good physical shape by reading articles on conditioning. You have to work out regularly. In the same way and for essentially the same reasons, data analysis has to be learned actively. It is crucial that you perform your own analysis. Simply reading about how it is done will not give you the functional understanding that makes statistics so useful. The exercises in this workbook are designed to do just that: give you actual training in data analysis.

- **Keep substance over method**. Whenever possible think about the substantive context of a problem. You may be asked to calculate a mean or standard deviation, for example. But what is important is not the numbers per se (although they do have to be correct) but rather what they say about the problem at hand. For example, instead of just writing, "The average is ten," you should write, "The average is ten thousand dollars," to keep firmly in mind that you are working on a concrete issue and not an abstract algebra problem.

■ **Be neat and orderly**. Yes, this advice sounds peevish. Yet we have found that a huge number of mistakes and misconceptions arise simply from disorderly note taking and hand calculations. It is always a good idea to have plenty of scrap paper handy and to work in a top-down fashion rather than jump all around the page putting intermediate calculations here and there in no logical order. It should be possible for you or anyone else to reconstruct your thought processes by following your calculations from beginning to end. That way errors and misunderstandings can be spotted and corrected.

■ **Don't trust the computer.** Many of the questions we ask can be answered only with the assistance of a computer, and we are the first to admit that computers are marvelous devices. But they have no ability to grasp what you mean to type and do not have the common sense to decipher what to you may be obvious. (We have stressed in the text on several occasions that a computer can only do what it is told and consequently will not make a mistake unless directed to do so.) So every time you turn on the computer, be prepared. Ahead of time ask yourself, "What do I need to find out? What procedure will give me the answers?" If you find yourself getting frustrated or something does not work no matter how many times you try, back off. Turn off the machine, go for a brief walk, rewrite your questions on a fresh piece of paper, and then go back to the system.

In these assignments we ask you to examine one variable at a time. The idea is to summarize a possibly large batch of numbers with a few indicators of a distribution's central tendency, variation, and shape. We have also appended a brief set of guidelines for preparing your own data for analysis.

Exercise 11–1. In this first exercise you should consider some of the basic terms that are key to understanding chapter 11. Some of these terms can sound too similar to differentiate or appear too complex to understand at first glance. For each pair of terms below, first define each term then explain the important differences between them.

a. Relative frequency and cumulative frequency

_____

_____

_____

b. Frequency and proportion

_____

_____

_____

c. Central tendency and dispersion

_____

_____

_____

d.   Range and interquartile range

_____

_____

_____

e.   Frequency distribution and normal distribution

_____

_____

_____

Exercise 11–2.   Measures of central tendency describe the typical value in a variable. Below you will find variables that might arise in political science research and a measure of central tendency. For each pairing explain why you think the selected measure would be appropriate or inappropriate. If you think it would be inappropriate, explain why you think a different measure would be a better choice. When answering the questions make sure to consider levels of measurement and the possibilities of outliers or skewed data.

a.   Variable: *flag colors*: indicates the color scheme of each nation's flag

Measure of central tendency: mean

_____

_____

b.   Variable: *marital status*: indicates whether respondent is single, married, separated, divorced, widow(er)

Measure of central tendency: mode

_____

_____

c.   Variable: *percent sixty-five*: indicates the percentage of citizens of each state age sixty-five or older.

Measure of central tendency: mean

_____

_____

d.   Variable: *annual household income*: dollar amount earned by each household in a year

Measure of central tendency: mean

_____

_____

e. Variable: *development*: indicates how developed a country is (developed, developing, underdeveloped)

Measure of central tendency: median

_____

_____

f. Variable: *rating*: indicates the pro-business rating earned by each U.S. senator from the U.S. Chamber of Commerce on a 100-point scale

Measure of central tendency: mode

_____

_____

Exercise 11–3. For this exercise you will use the sample data in table 11–1.

TABLE 11–1
**Hypothetical Miles
per Gallon for Large SUVs**

i	MPG, Sample 1	MPG, Sample 2
1	5	1
2	5	4
3	5	5
4	5	5
5	5	10

a. Calculate the mean, median, and mode for each sample.

_____

b. Calculate the range and standard deviation for each sample.

_____

c. Why is it important to calculate and consider measures of dispersion alongside measures of central tendency?

_____

_____

Exercise 11–4. The 2008 National Election Study posed the following question: "Some people believe that we should spend much less money for defense. Others feel that defense spending should be greatly increased. Where would you place yourself on this scale or haven't you thought much about this?"[1] Here is a tally of responses to the question:

Greatly decrease	1:	82
	2:	82
	3:	128
	4:	280
	5:	210
	6:	128
Greatly increase	7:	93
Don't know		164

Source: Data compiled from the American National Election Studies (http://www.electionstudies.org), *The 2008 National Election Study* (data set).

a. In the space below create a frequency distribution for the responses that includes the raw numbers, the relative frequencies (or proportions or percentages), the valid relative frequencies (or proportions or percentages), and the cumulative proportions or percentages. (Treat "don't know" responses as missing data.)

_____

_____

b. What is the modal category?

_____

_____

Exercise 11–5. This exercise is intended to help you familiarize yourself with the statistical package you will be using in class. The focus of this exercise is not on using or interpreting statistics but on introducing you to commonly used tools and commands that you will be using on a regular basis. You will be using the "States" data set available on the Web site. On the Web site you will find the file in multiple formats, including comma-separated format, which can be used to create a file for just about any software package. You should use the package your instructor chooses.

The first step is to locate and save a copy of the "states" file. I suggest that you use a memory stick or e-mail the file to yourself if you are working on a computer in a lab. Saving your work frequently while working with data is a very good idea. I suggest that you get in the practice of saving multiple iterations of data files. For example, after working on a file for twenty minutes or so, or before making big changes to a data set, I will save

---

[1] The American National Election Studies (http://www.electionstudies.org), *The 2008 National Election Study* (data set), Ann Arbor, University of Michigan, Center for Political Studies [producer and distributor].

a file as a new iteration. If working with the "states" file, I might call the first save "states1." Then, after working for a while, I would save a new copy called "states2," then "states3," and so on. Thus I will have saved a history of my work. If I should realize that I have made a mistake somewhere along the line, I can go back to the last save previous to the mistake without having to start all over.

Now that you have the "states" file open and saved, it is time to begin. Complete each step below. Please remember that while every software package has slightly different names for commands, the basic steps you are taking below are common to all software packages. You might just have to poke around a bit and find the correct command.

a. Visual inspection

Before beginning any project it is wise to inspect the data so you understand what you have. The "states" data have one row for each of the fifty states and a column for each variable. Take a look at the kinds of variables that are available in the dataset. You will see that there is a wide array of information in the file about the states.

b. Select cases

The first step is to reduce the size of the dataset. We want to work with only the non-southern states that gave Mitt Romney greater than 45 percent of the presidential vote in 2012. Delete the southern states from the data using the *South* variable. Delete states that gave Romney less than or equal to 45 percent of the presidential vote in 2012.

c. Sort cases

Sort the states by population and list the five most populous states here:

1. _____   2. _____   3. _____   4. _____   5. _____

Sort cases by religiosity and persons over sixty-five and list the five states that were most religious in order from highest percentage of persons over age sixty-five to lowest here:

(*Hint:* 3 is the most religious and 1 is the least on the variable *religiosity*):

1. _____   2. _____   3. _____   4. _____   5. _____

d. Create a new variable

Create a new dichotomous variable that indicates whether a state had more than 60 percent turnout in the 2012 presidential election. A dichotomous variable is a variable with two categories. It is often advantageous to code a dichotomous variable with the values of 1 and 0, where 1 means that the characteristic measured by the variable is present and 0 means that the characteristic is absent. For this variable, which you will call *highturnout*, use a 1 when the characteristic is present (high turnout / >65 percent) and a 0 when the characteristic is absent (not high turnout / <=65 percent).

e. Create a pie chart that demonstrates the proportion of high-turnout states to low-turnout states.

f. Label the pie chart to indicate greater than 65 percent and less than or equal to 65 percent turnout. Give the pie chart a descriptive title.

g. Create a table that includes the mean vote percentage for Romney and Obama in 2012 in the selected states.

h. Give the table a descriptive title.

i. Copy and paste your pie chart, table, and associated titles into a single document to turn in with this page.

Exercise 11-6. Using the hypothetical data in table 11–2, calculate the sample variance and sample standard deviation. Next, calculate the population variance and the population standard deviation using the same data. After completing your calculations, explain in plain English why the answers are different for the sample and population equations. How and why are the formulae different?

TABLE 11–2

Political Events Attended

Respondent Identification	Number of Political Events Attended in Last Year
1	4
2	3
3	0
4	1
5	7
6	3
7	1
8	0
9	5
10	1

Exercise 11-7. Use the data in table 11–3 to answer the following questions about central tendency and dispersion. You will need to think about which statistics best represent the data.

TABLE 11–3

Military Spending 2014, Select Countries

Country	Military Spending[a]
United States	581
China	129
Saudi Arabia	81
Russia	70
UK	62
Japan	48
India	45
Germany	44
Brazil	32
Italy	24
Israel	23
Australia	23

Source: International Institute for Strategic Studies, *The Military Balance 2015* (London: Routledge, 2015).

[a] Military spending in billions, rounded to a whole number.

a. What is the mean military spending?

    _____

b. What is the median military spending?

    _____

c. What is the trimmed mean military spending? (Cut one value from each end.)

    _____

d. Comment on the difference between the mean, the median, and the trimmed mean in this context. Which do you think is the best value to use to describe central tendency?

    _____

    _____

    _____

e. What is the maximum value, the minimum value, and the range?

    _____

f. What is the first quartile (Q1)? _____ The third quartile (Q3)? _____

    The interquartile range (IQR)? _____

g. Which measure of dispersion is the more appropriate choice for these data, the range or the interquartile range? Why?

HELPFUL HINTS

Online Statistical Programs

One of the benefits of the Internet is the wide availability of statistical programs. Many allow you to enter small amounts of data such as are found in these exercises. The programs vary greatly in content and quality, but you can use them to obtain many introductory statistical analyses. Two examples are listed below.

■ Larry Green's Applet Page, Calculating One Variable Statistics, available at http://www .ltcconline.net/greenl/java/Statistics/One VariableStatistics/OneVariableStatistics .htm. Provides the mean, median, mode, maximum, minimum, range, variance, and standard deviation.

■ Statistical Applets, available at http://www .assumption.edu/users/avadum/applets/ applets.html. Calculates mean, standard deviation (calculated two ways), variance, sum of squares, median, minimum, maximum, 25th percentile, and 75th percentile.

As abundant and easy to use as these resources are, pay attention to these potential problems:

■ Your instructor may want you to use a single program. There is a good reason for this requirement: not all software computes statistics in the same way. Your answers may be valid according to one program but not another. Trying to sort these matters out can be extremely difficult.

■ As the text alludes to in several places and as we mentioned earlier, some statistics and most graphs can be calculated correctly in different ways. For example, the text acquires the standard deviation by obtaining the square root of the sum of squares divided by $N - 1$. Many textbooks, however, instruct you to divide by simply N.

If the number of cases is not large, the two versions of the standard deviation will differ. So if you use one program and someone else uses another, your results may not agree.

■ Most of the sites use Java applets, which means your browser has to support Java. Some applets take forever and a day to load, especially if the connection speed is slow.

■ Internet sites come and go. Make sure you will not need to return to one to finish an assignment.

■ Commercial sites may require you to register and/or pay a fee to use their software.

In spite of these possible pitfalls, the Internet can be an excellent source for supplementing your introduction to applied statistics.

Exercise 11–8. Table 11–4 reports the number of executions in states that executed prisoners in 2014.

TABLE 11–4
States That Executed Prisoners, 2014

State	Executions
Arizona	1
Florida	8
Georgia	2
Missouri	10
Ohio	1
Oklahoma	3
Texas	10

Source: Data are from Death Penalty Information Center, "Execution List 2014," http://www.deathpenaltyinfo.org/execution-list-2014.

Compute the following descriptive statistics, treating these data as the *population* of all states that executed prisoners in 2014:

a. Mean

b. Variance

c. Standard deviation

_____

d. Interpret the mean and standard deviation in a single sentence that describes execution data.

_____

Exercise 11–9. Table 11–5 reports the minimum wage in seven states.

TABLE 11–5

State Minimum Wage as of February 24, 2015

State	Minimum Wage
Alaska	8.75
Colorado	8.23
Idaho	7.25
Illinois	8.25
Nebraska	8.00
Rhode Island	9.00
Virginia	7.25

Source: Data are from National Conference of State Legislatures, "2015 Minimum Wages by State," http://www.ncsl.org/research/labor-and-employment/state-minimum-wage-chart.aspx.

Compute the following descriptive statistics, treating these data as a *sample* of all states:

a. Mean

_____

b. Variance

_____

c. Standard deviation

_____

d. Interpret the mean and standard deviation in a single sentence that describes the minimum wage data.

_____

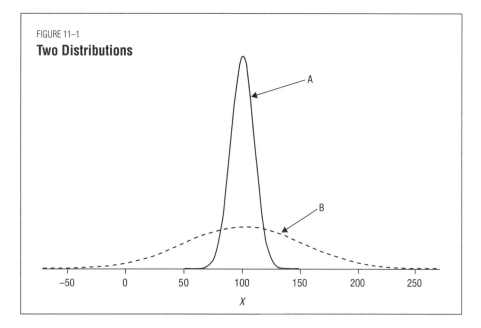

FIGURE 11–1
Two Distributions

Exercise 11–10. Figure 11–1 contains two distributions, A and B.

a. Which distribution has the greater variation? _____

b. Which distribution has the smaller standard deviation? _____

c. How do measures of central tendency for distributions A and B differ, if they differ at all?

_____

d. What are the mean and the median of distribution A? _____

e. What are the mean and the median of distribution B? _____

Exercise 11–11. During the 2004 presidential campaign, there was a lot of discussion about who benefited from the tax cuts initiated and signed into law by the George W. Bush administration. Senator John Kerry said, "George Bush's only economic plan is lavish tax breaks for those at the top." President Bush asserted proudly, "I have twice led the United States Congress to pass historic tax relief for the American people." Part of the argument turned on dollar amounts received by different groups. A White House news release claimed, "Under the President's proposal to speed up tax relief, 92 million taxpayers would receive, on average, a tax cut of $1,083 in 2003."[2] Yet one of the president's critics wrote, "The average working family would get about $289."[3] Assuming both sides are telling the truth, how do you suppose they could reach such different conclusions? You will not be able to provide a definitive answer, but your knowledge of summary statistics should give you a good idea.

---

[2] The White House, "Fact Sheet: President Bush Taking Action to Strengthen America's Economy," January 2003, http://georgewbush-whitehouse.archives.gov/news/releases/2003/01/20030107.html.

[3] Kathryn Casa, "The Elephant in the Room," *CounterPunch*, http://www.counterpunch.org/casa01292003.html.

_____
_____
_____
_____
_____
_____
_____
_____

Exercise 11–12.   Define as clearly as possible the following statistics. Write a formula if you wish, but try to explain each term in plain language as well.

a.   The sample standard deviation

_____
_____
_____
_____
_____

b.   The median

_____
_____
_____
_____
_____

c.   The mode

_____
_____
_____
_____
_____

d. The trimmed mean

_____

_____

_____

_____

_____

e. The interquartile range

_____

_____

_____

_____

_____

Exercise 11–13. There is a gender gap in the United States when it comes to wages. In 2013 women earned 78 percent of men's wages nationwide. In this exercise you will attempt to create your own box plot that summarizes and explores the sample of state wage gaps in table 11–6.

TABLE 11–6

Percentage of Men's Wages Earned by State, 2013

State	Wage Gap[a]
New York	86
Florida	84
Nevada	83
Oregon	80
Missouri	79
South Carolina	78
Iowa	78
Mississippi	77
Alabama	76
Utah	70
Louisiana	66

Source: Data are from the American Association of University Women, "The Gender Pay Gap by State and Congressional District," http://www.aauw.org/resource/gender-pay-gap-by-state-and-congressional-district/.

[a] Median earnings of women working full time compared to men, 2013

Follow the steps below to create your box plot.

1. Find the maximum and minimum, the first and third quartiles, the interquartile range (IQR), and the median.

   Maximum: _____ Minimum:_____ First quartile: _____ Third quartile: _____

   Interquartile Range: _____ Median: _____

2. Draw a horizontal line to indicate the scale of the variable. Mark off intervals of the variable. Be sure to fully label the scale.
3. Above the line, say about half an inch or so, draw a small vertical line to indicate the median. It should correspond to the appropriate value on the scale.
4. Draw short vertical lines of the same size above the scale to indicate Q1 and Q3.
5. Sketch a rectangle with the two quartiles (Q1 and Q3) at the ends. The median will be in the box somewhere. The height of the rectangle does not matter.
6. Calculate 1.5 times the interquartile range: _____
7. Calculate the lower whisker. The lower whisker is the *maximum* of either (1) the minimum of the variable *or* (2) 1.5 times the IQR. In symbols, the lower whisker equals the maximum of (minimum[variable], 1.5 × IQR). Call this quantity LW for short.
8. Draw a line to represent LW at the left end (Q1) of the box.
9. Do the same for the upper whisker. This time, however, you take the *minimum* of either (1) the maximum of the variable *or* (2) 1.5 times the IQR. More succinctly, the upper whisker is the lesser of the maximum value of the variable, or 1.5 × IQR. Call the result UW.
10. Draw a line from the third quartile (Q3) to the point UW.
11. Place points or symbols to indicate the actual location of extreme values. These should be labeled with the observation name or number.
12. Give the graph a title and properly label the *x*-axis.

Title: _____

APPENDIX TO CHAPTER 11

Preparing Data for Analysis

You may at some point be asked to collect data on your own. The textbook and the workbook provide examples of how the information can be organized for analysis by hand or computer. Here are a few specific tips that might speed up the process and help you avoid common mistakes.

Think of this step as more than just organizing and cleaning the data so that they can be easily analyzed by hand or (more likely) computer—it has theoretical importance as well. Among other tasks, this process requires checking for and correcting errors; looking for inconsistencies (for example, a man who reports having had an abortion); recoding or changing recorded information to make it more analytically tractable; combing or separating categories of nominal variables; and determining what are to be considered valid responses. These efforts are often invisible because research organizations (such as the one that conducts the National Election Studies) do much of the work before releasing the information to others. But even so, end users have to know what has been done and frequently may need to make additional adjustments, such as deciding what to do with "don't know" versus "not interested" responses. Moreover, if you are collecting statistics from scratch, you have to put the information into a layout that facilitates tabulation and analysis. This process has important implications because at the end of the day these are the actual numbers used in constructing, testing, and modifying hypotheses and models. You would be amazed at how supposedly innocuous technical details can affect substantive conclusions.[4]

To further explore this, let's use the topic of income inequality as a concrete example. A general statement of one hypothesis is, "The greater the degree of union membership, the more 'income equality' a nation will have." Suppose we have collected some data to investigate this hypothesis. Look at table 11–1 in the textbook, which shows data for a sample of twenty-one nations.[5] The table contains operational indicators of income inequality and socioeconomic measures.

Note first that the table comprises what we call a data matrix, which, as we explained in the text, is a rectangular array in which the rows contain data for individual observations (one row per case) and columns contain variables. Australia, for instance, has a Gini index score of 35.2, a union density of 23.1 percent, and so forth. The Gini index variable is just one way of measuring income inequality—and in fact there are even many different methods used to calculate the Gini index. The slight variations in these measures could lead one to make slightly different conclusions about income inequality. Similar choices must be made when measuring other complex concepts. While most studies make these kinds of choices, they are sometimes not readily apparent.

- **Recording numbers.** Most computer programs insist that you enter numbers *without commas*. So, for example, 5,000 would be typed 5000. Moreover, *do not* use symbols such as the dollar ($) or percent (%) signs.

- **Plus and minus signs.** If the original data contain negative values, they have to be entered with a minus sign. Positive values are always entered *without* a plus sign.

- **Precision.** We use at most two decimal places, mainly because the original sources contained only that many. Precision can be a tricky problem in statistical analysis. On one hand, in long, involved calculations, so-called round-off errors (the rounding of decimal numbers during intermediate steps) can rapidly accumulate and lead to results that differ from those based on exact numbers. On the other hand, when you present data tables to others, one or two decimal places is usually sufficient.

---

[4] Clifford Clogg shows how the treatment of "don't know" responses to a question about the judicial system's toughness on criminals affects substantive conclusions. Clifford Clogg, "Using Association Models in Sociological Research: Some Examples," *American Journal of Sociology* 88 (July 1982): 114–34.

[5] The data in table 11–1 constitute a partial random and judgmental sample, not a purely random sample of the world's nation-states. For the sake of simplicity, however, we treat the numbers as if they were a truly random sample from an infinite population.

- **Labels versus names.** To facilitate computer analysis, each variable has a short label or tag. Most computer programs require relatively brief names or abbreviations, like the ones used here, but they can often handle separately entered longer descriptive labels. Note, however, that if a data matrix is to be published, every effort should be made to assign intelligible names to the variables. Otherwise, readers can easily lose the meanings of the tags.

- **Category combinations.** Sometimes you have to combine categories to achieve an optimal number of cases. For example, we might assign New Zealand to Asia and Morocco and Egypt to the Middle East to avoid having categories with just one or two observations. The key is to make the assignments as explicit as possible so that others can understand and, if need be, challenge or modify them.

- **Recoding.** It may or may not be necessary, depending on software, to recode text to numeric values. If we were using a variable that captures the level of development, this variable could be coded in more than one way. *Status*, for instance, could be simply reported as "developed" or "developing" or we could choose numeric codes 1 and 5, respectively, to stand for the substantive categories. The designation is arbitrary; we could use 1 and 2 or 50 and 500 or any other two numbers. Since development status is a nominal variable, the numbers do not have an intrinsic quantitative meaning. But, surprisingly perhaps, it is legitimate to make use of these arbitrary numbers in some statistical procedures. We show how in chapter 13.

- **Missing data.** What do you do when data for a particular observation are not available because they were not collected or reported? This is the missing data problem. Imagine that a respondent did not answer one question on a survey form. Despite this, there is information for the remaining questions. When entered into a dataset we must indicate the missing information with an indicator—often 999 or some other repeating number or character, such as a single period. When our computer program encounters this symbol, it deletes the case for a particular procedure involving that variable and continues with its work. The result would be based on one fewer case. Do the respondents with and without reported values differ in any systematic ways? It is hard to tell, which explains why a lot of thought has to go into collecting and preparing data for analysis. Each of these seemingly trivial matters can have significant implications.[6] A rule of thumb is that if 20 percent or more of your cases have missing values for a variable, you might consider dropping it or finding one that has more complete information.

- **Error and consistency checking.** Always check for errors and inconsistencies. In many instances preliminary descriptive and exploratory analyses will alert you to the possibility of errors in the data. But this is not always the case, so if you are collecting data by hand, check and recheck the numbers.

- **Weights.** When certain sampling designs are used to collect the data, it may be necessary to adjust the numbers to reflect over- or underrepresentation of certain groups. This is not an issue in the comparative data we used to analyze levels of democratization, but many academic polls contain weighted data. The 2004 National Election Study does, and one would need to take care of the weighting in an analysis. If you download data from the Internet, always check. (Most, but alas not all, software allows you to identify a weighted variable and will adjust the data for you.) In this book, however, weighting is never a problem.

---

[6] An enormous amount of thought has gone into the problem of missing data. For a review of a few statistical solutions, see Joseph L. Schafer and John W. Graham, "Missing Data: Our View of the State of the Art," *Psychological Methods* 7 (2002): 147–77.

CHAPTER 12

Statistical Inference

Chapter 12 expands on the introduction to statistics found in chapter 11, moving from basic statistical concepts like central tendency and dispersion to more complex hypothesis testing and confidence intervals. While chapter 11 explains how statistics can be used to explore data, chapter 12 focuses on making inferences using statistics. In this chapter in the workbook you will be asked to use your new statistical skills to analyze data to answer questions.

Exercise 12–1. For this exercise you should refer to the definition and explanation of type I and type II errors in chapter 12, then think about the following hypothetical research project. The 2014 midterm election was a low-turnout election, with just 36.4 percent of eligible voters casting ballots—the lowest turnout rate in seventy years.[1] In response to such low voter participation, the U.S. government has announced a $100 million grant to fund a program to increase voter turnout. As a brilliant political science student, you feel certain that offering civics classes to voting-eligible adults would improve turnout rates. You think that voters would surely turn out at a higher rate if they only knew how vital participation is to democracy. To support your application for the $100 million, you use your new methodological skills to test the hypothesis that likelihood of voting increases after taking a civics class.

In the space provided below, explain the consequences of making a type I error and a type II error when testing your hypothesis about the relationship between civics classes and the likelihood of voting.

_____

_____

_____

_____

_____

_____

---

[1] Domenico Montanaro, Rachel Wellford, and Simone Pathe, "2014 Midterm Election Turnout Lowest in 70 Years," *PBS News Hour*, November 10, 2014, http://www.pbs.org/newshour/updates/2014-midterm-election-turnout-lowest-in-70-years/.

Exercise 12–2. Have you considered why we can use sample statistics for any variable? How can we use inferential statistics with a ratio-level variable such as income, an ordinal variable measuring education, or a dichotomous variable measuring gender? The answer is that each variable is normally distributed in its sampling distribution. For this exercise you will explore the sampling distribution for a variable that is binomial: a coin flip. It is binomial because it has only two categories, heads and tails. While you cannot ever observe a sampling distribution because it is created with an infinite number of samples—which we can of course never complete—you can begin to see how a sampling distribution might look. For this exercise you will need a coin. Below you will record the results of ten series of coin flips, with ten flips in each series. You will flip the coin ten times and record the total number of heads you observe in the space marked Series 1. You will then proceed to flip the coin ten more times and record your observations for Series 2, and so on. Once you have recorded all your observations, use a bar graph (review chapter 11) to visually display the results from the ten series (the number of heads observed in each series) in the space to the right. How does tossing coins demonstrate the concept of the sampling distribution?

Example: Seven heads (I flipped my coin ten times and counted seven heads, so I wrote seven in the blank.)

Series 1: _____ heads

Series 2: _____ heads

Series 3: _____ heads

Series 4: _____ heads

Series 5: _____ heads

Series 6: _____ heads

Series 7: _____ heads

Series 8: _____ heads

Series 9: _____ heads

Series 10: _____ heads

Exercise 12–3. Many of the statistics in chapter 12 rely on the concept of statistical significance. To assert statistical significance one can compare a test or observed value to a critical value from a distribution, such as the normal or student's t distribution. In appendix B of the textbook you will find a table containing critical values from the t distribution. For each set of circumstances below indicate whether the observed value is sufficiently great to assert statistical significance.

1. t_{obs} = 2.1, 15 degrees of freedom, two-tailed test, 95 percent confidence level: _____

2. t_{obs} = 1.9, 24 degrees of freedom, two-tailed test, 90 percent confidence level: _____

3. t_{obs} = 2.5, 11 degrees of freedom, one-tailed test, 99 percent confidence level: _____

4. t_{obs} = 1.5, 30 degrees of freedom, one-tailed test, 95 percent confidence level: _____

5. t_{obs} = 2.6, 4 degrees of freedom, two-tailed test, 90 percent confidence level: _____

6. t_{obs} = 2.01, 50 degrees of freedom, two-tailed test, 95 percent confidence level: _____

7. t_{obs} = 2.4, 800 degrees of freedom, one-tailed test, 99 percent confidence level: _____

8. t_{obs} = 3.5, 19 degrees of freedom, two-tailed test, 99.8 percent confidence level: _____

9. t_{obs} = 1.9, 7 degrees of freedom, one-tailed test, 99 percent confidence level: _____

10. t_{obs} = 4.0, 21 degrees of freedom, two-tailed test, 99.9 percent confidence level: _____

Exercise 12–4. The next set of questions is designed to help you get used to translating a political claim into a statistical hypothesis that can be tested.

According to the U.S. Census Bureau, "The nation's public school districts spent an average of $8,701 per student on elementary and secondary education in fiscal year 2005, up 5 percent from the previous year."[2] A staff member for a candidate for governor has conducted a random sample of fifteen school districts and found that the mean spending level is only $8,000 per pupil. The candidate is using this finding to support his charge that the incumbent is weak on education. The newspaper you work for wants to know whether the difference between the population mean ($8,701) and the sample mean ($8,000) suggests that on the whole your state spends less on education than the rest of the country or if the results are likely due to sampling error.

a. Write a null hypothesis for this problem.

_____

_____

b. Write an alternative hypothesis. (*Hint:* Think carefully about the context. The candidate's argument is that the state spends less than the rest of the country.)

_____

_____

c. What statistical test would you use to evaluate the null hypothesis? Why?

_____

_____

_____

---

[2] U.S. Census Bureau, "Public Education Finances," Census Project Update, http://www.census.gov/mp/www/cpu/factoftheday/010196.html.

d. What would be the appropriate sampling distribution? Why?

_____

_____

_____

Exercise 12–5.   The United States has hosted foreign heads of state or heads of government from forty-nine countries who have made 116 speeches before Congress. Table 12–1 includes data on those countries whose leaders have made four or more appearances. We will assume that this table includes the *full population of appearances* to keep the number of cases small for the calculation. Using the data in table 12–1, calculate a *z* score and use the *z* score to find the probability of leaders from a country delivering seven or more speeches before Congress.

TABLE 12–1

Number of Speeches to Congress by Foreign Heads of State of Selected Countries

Country	Number of Speeches
United Kingdom	8
Israel	8
Mexico	7
France	7
Italy	6
South Korea	6
Ireland	6
Germany	5
India	4

Source: Data are from Mike Nudelman, "Only One Other Person Addressed Congress as Many Times as Netanyahu," *Business Insider*, March 3, 2015, http://www.businessinsider.com/only-one-other-person-addressed-congress-as-many-times-as-netanyahu-2015-3.

a. Draw the normal distribution here. Label information as you go to keep track of everything and shade the area of interest under the curve. Include the X and Z scales.

b. Calculate the mean and standard deviation.

_____

c. Calculate the *z* score.

_____

d. What is the probability of leaders from a country delivering seven or more speeches before Congress?

_____

Exercise 12–6. For this exercise you will need to consult appendices A and B in the text. For each of the following questions, use the appropriate appendix to find the answer.

a. Find the probability associated with a *z* score of 1.20.

_____

b. Find the probability associated with a *z* score of 2.25.

_____

c. Find the *z* score associated with a probability of .2912.

_____

d. Find the *z* score associated with a probability of .0062.

_____

e. Find a *t* score using a two-tailed test, an alpha level of .05, and ten degrees of freedom.

_____

f. Find a *t* score using a one-tailed test, an alpha level of .01, and fifteen degrees of freedom.

_____

g. Why is the largest probability listed in appendix A .5000?

_____

_____

h. Why do the probabilities in appendix A get smaller as the *z* scores get larger?

_____

_____

i. Why are *t* scores larger with fewer degrees of freedom and smaller with more degrees of freedom?

_____

_____

j. Find the probability associated with a *z* score of 1.96. Find *t* scores using the two-tailed test, a .05 alpha level, and an infinite degree of freedom. What is the important relationship among these answers?

_____

_____

_____

_____

TABLE 12–2

Demonstration Data for *t*-Tests

i	*x*
1	4
2	3
3	6
4	0
5	2
6	3

Exercise 12–7. There are many different ways to test a hypothesis. In chapter 12 the authors explain how to use a two-sided and a one-sided *t*-test. In the space following, please explain the circumstances under which you would use a one-sided *t*-test and a two-sided *t*-test. Next, use the hypothetical sample data in table 12–2 to perform a sample *t*-test testing the sample mean against a test value of 1. Use the 95 percent confidence level and calculate the critical *t* value using both a one-sided and two-sided test. How do these calculations illustrate the difference between the two tests?

_____

_____

_____

TABLE 12–3

Bills Written by Members of Congress in One Session of Congress

Observation	Bills Written
1	4
2	10
3	1
4	3
5	8
6	7
7	5
8	2
9	3
10	5

_____

_____

_____

Exercise 12–8. Suppose you have collected sample data on the number of bills written by members of Congress in a single session of Congress. Using the data in table 12–3, use a *t*-test to determine whether the following null hypothesis is correct: The observed mean in your sample data is not statistically significantly different from 5.5. Use the two-tailed test and the 95 percent confidence level when answering this question. Do you accept or reject the null hypothesis? Why would you use a two-tailed test?

_____

_____

_____

Exercise 12–9. Imagine that you have access to sample data from the U.S. State Department about the amount of money different nations spend on educational programs designed to foster goodwill with citizens from other countries. While you would prefer full access to the data, the State Department agrees to tell you only the population mean and provide you with a sample of the population data. You reluctantly agree, pending verification that the sample data is representative of the population data. The population mean is $13.4 million. The hypothetical sample data to which you have access is listed in table 12–4. Use a *t*-test to determine whether the data to which you have access is representative of the population data by testing the mean of your data against the population mean provided by the State Department. You should use a two-tailed test and a 95 percent confidence level. Explain how a *t*-test could help you decide whether using the sample data is sufficient.

TABLE 12–4

Millions of Dollars Spent Fostering Goodwill

Country	Millions of Dollars
Brazil	8
Canada	16
Denmark	11
Ghana	5
Kuwait	6
India	9
Malaysia	1
South Africa	8
South Korea	10
United Kingdom	18

Exercise 12–10. The calculations for difference of means *t*- and *z*-tests include several parts, including the difference of the means, the standard deviation, and the sample size. Suppose that another student in the class does not understand how the difference of the means, the standard deviation, or the sample size affects the *t* and *z* values when using a *t*-test or a *z*-test. In the spaces provided, please explain how changes in each affect the *t* and *z* values and the likelihood of finding statistical significance.

a. A larger standard deviation

b. A larger sample size

c. A larger difference of the means

_____

_____

_____

d. What is the standard error of the mean? What does it tell us about our data, and why is it important in testing hypotheses?

_____

_____

_____

_____

_____

_____

Exercise 12–11.   We can use a confidence interval to determine the range in which we expect to find the population mean, given a certain level of confidence. The range we find using this statistic varies based on the values of the standard deviation, the sample size, and the confidence level. In the following problems you will manipulate the values used in a *population confidence interval* to learn how changes in these values affect the size of the confidence interval.

Population Confidence Interval

Calculate the population confidence interval with a sample mean of 5, a sample size of 500, a confidence level of 95 percent, and a population standard deviation of 2.

_____

_____

_____

Change in Standard Deviation

In the first step, you calculated the population confidence interval with a mean of 5, a sample size of 500, a confidence level of 95 percent, and a standard deviation of 2. In this step you are going to analyze the effect of changing the size of the standard deviation. This time, use a population standard deviation of 4. How does a larger (smaller) standard deviation affect the calculation of a confidence interval? Why is this so?

_____

_____

_____

_____

Change in Sample Size

In the first step, you calculated the population confidence interval with a mean of 5, a sample size of 500, a confidence level of 95 percent, and a standard deviation of 2. Now use the same standard deviation and confidence level but use a sample size of 1,000. How does a larger (smaller) sample size affect the calculation of a confidence interval? Why is this so?

_____

_____

_____

_____

Change in Confidence Level

In the first step, you calculated the population confidence interval with a mean of 5, a sample size of 500, a confidence level of 95 percent, and a standard deviation of 2. Calculate the population confidence interval with a mean of 5, a sample size of 500, a confidence level of 90 percent, and a standard deviation of 2. How does a larger (smaller) confidence level affect the calculation of a confidence interval? Why is this so?

_____

_____

_____

_____

Exercise 12–12. In chapter 12 the authors explain how you can use a confidence interval to test a hypothesis. Imagine that you are working on a research project on the effectiveness of Twitter as a political tool. As part of this project, you have hypothesized that the typical politician has nine followers at the beginning of a campaign. Using the hypothetical sample data in table 12–5, where i represents the rows of data and x represents the number of followers each candidate has at the beginning of a campaign, calculate a sample confidence interval. Decide whether you should accept or reject your hypothesis and explain why you would do so. Use the .05 level and a two-tailed test.

TABLE 12–5

Twitter Followers

i	x
1	12
2	3
3	6
4	7
5	5
6	10
7	6

_____

_____

_____

_____

_____

Exercise 12–13. It is time to see how statistics software tests a hypothesis. Consider an estimate of life expectancy. A classmate has estimated that life expectancy worldwide is probably about seventy-two years. You will use a *t*-test to determine if there is a statistical difference between the classmate's estimated life expectancy and the real life expectancy.

Null Hypothesis H_0: life expectancy = 72

Alternative Hypothesis H_A: life expectancy ≠ 72

For this exercise you will be using the "Human Development" data set available on the Web site. The data were collected by the United Nations and used to create an index of human development in each country based on life expectancy, income, and educational attainment. Open the file and select the *life expectancy* variable.

a. You will use 72 as the test value in your hypothesis test. In other words, you will enter 72 in the statistical package *t*-test and test 72 against the mean of the *life expectancy* variable. Report your observed *t* score on the line below. Then explain whether there is a statistically significant difference between the values and how you came to that decision. Use a 95 percent confidence level (two-tail test).

_____

_____

_____

Exercise 12–14.   In this exercise you will be using a software package in testing a hypothesis.

Imagine that during a lecture on voting behavior your professor claimed that despite the widespread use of social media, only 20 percent of people use social media to discuss politics. As a student of data analysis, you have decided to test this claim. Using the "Social Vote" data set, test the following hypotheses using the *t*-test for proportions method.

Null Hypothesis H_0: proportion of those who share political information on social media = .2

Alternative Hypothesis H_A: proportion of those who share political information on social media ≠ .2

You will test the hypothesis using the *PIAL3* variable in the "social vote" data set available on the Web site. This data set was collected by the Pew Research Center and includes data about how people used social media during the 2012 presidential election. The *PIAL3* variable includes respondents' answers to the following question: "Have you let other people know who you voted for, or who you plan to vote for, in this year's election by posting that information on a social networking site such as Facebook or Twitter?"

a. Use a software package to open the social vote data file and use the package to find the proportion of 1s to 0s and the standard deviation for the *PIAL3* variable. Report the answers here:

_____

b. Calculate a *t* score using a test of a proportion as outlined in the text. Use the proportion and standard deviation you calculated in part a using a 95 percent confidence level and a two-tail test.

_____

c. Do you accept the professor's statement as true?

_____

Exercise 12–15. In this exercise you will use software to find a sample confidence interval. Open the "State Legislatures" file and take a look at the *percent* variable. This variable measures the percentage of each state's legislature comprised of female legislators. For this problem we want to compute a 95 percent confidence interval (two-tail test) using this sample data. Compute the 95 percent confidence interval and then answer the following questions.

a. What is the mean and standard deviation for the *percent* variable?

_____

b. What is the value of the standard error of the mean in the confidence interval?

_____

c. What is the confidence interval?

_____

CHAPTER 13

Investigating Relationships between Two Variables

Chapter 13 takes up the analysis of relationships between two variables. Two variables are statistically related when values of the observations for one variable are associated with values of the observations for the other. This chapter gives you a chance to investigate several aspects of two-variable relationships, including strength, direction or shape, and statistical significance.

We mention throughout the textbook that plenty of career opportunities exist for political scientists who have a reasonable understanding of quantitative methods. So if you know a little about cross-tabulations, regression analysis, and statistical inference, you may find jobs waiting for you in campaigns, government, consulting firms, industry, and a host of other areas. But experience tells us that in almost every instance employers look for well-trained social scientists who can also clearly, succinctly, and forcefully explain numerical procedures and results to people who do not have much knowledge of (and, frankly, not much interest in) these topics. This ability becomes particularly valuable when someone asks, "Is this an important finding, one I should pay attention to, or can I ignore it?" Hence, we encourage you to think carefully about the answers to the questions posed here and in other chapters.

Here we offer some advice for translating statistical results into accessible language:

- **Before responding to the question (or submitting a report to your boss), consider what is being asked**. In the real world, people want answers expressed in real-world terms. You have been told that a regression coefficient, for example, can be interpreted as the slope of a line or as indicating how much Y changes for each unit increase or decrease in X. An r measures goodness of fit. But for many people, explanations expressed in those terms might as well be gibberish. It is essential, then, that you make sense of statistical terms by placing them in a specific substantive context. Regression and correlation coefficients indicate how and how strongly one thing is related to another. That's the importance of such coefficients. So make sure that you talk about variables, not equations or Greek letters or abstract symbols. For example, write "Income is related to attitudes on taxation," not "X is related to Y."

- **Go even further to explain the nature of interconnections**. Yes, income is correlated with opinions. But how? You might add, "The wealthier people are, the more they favor cutting taxes, but even the lower and middle classes want some degree of tax relief." This statement is much more informative to a nonstatistician than the statement, "There's a positive correlation."

- **We have suggested numerous times that the definitions of variables determine how we interpret the phenomena under consideration.** People want to know if there is a meaningful difference between A and B, or they want to understand how strongly X and Y are connected. Numbers alone won't do the job. Only the names and meanings of the variables will. So don't write something like, "There is a difference of ten (or a difference of ten units)." The difference is in what units? Dollars? Years? Pounds? Percentages?

- **In this same vein, the measurement scales of variables are critically important.** They should be one of the first things you look for and understand. In some cases the meaning of the categories or the intervals will be obvious or intuitive, as in "years of formal schooling." In other instances a scale may present more subtle explanatory difficulties. Take income, a variable we discuss several times in the text. In many cases the scale is just "dollars," so "$1,000" has a clear meaning. In other instances a variable may be measured in thousands, millions, or even billions of dollars. (That is, "$10" may stand for "$10 million.") It is important that you know exactly which scale is being used. After all, a change of ten means one thing when we are talking about simple dollars and quite another when the scale is millions or billions. And complicating matters even further, social scientists often measure variables on abstract or artificial scales. ("Where would you place yourself on this ten-point thermometer of feelings about the president?") If one person's score is seven and another's is five, the scores differ. But how important in the world of politics is this difference? As we emphasize below, it is only possible to give a reasoned judgment; there will seldom be a clearly right or wrong answer.

■ **You can help yourself by keeping track of measures of central tendency and variability**. If most respondents in a study have values near the mean or median, then one person whose score is two standard deviations away may be unusual and warrant further investigation. Was the individual's score measured correctly? Is he or she an "extremist?" The two interpretations, which have vastly different substantive implications, can be adjudicated only with thought and perhaps further research.

■ **Don't let one or two measures (for example, chi-square, *r*) do all your interpretative work.** Instead, try to examine the data as a whole. If you have a contingency table, look for patterns of association within the table's body. Compare different categories of the response patterns. For example, individuals at the high and low ends of a scale often differ greatly in their attitudes. Those in the middle may be more homogeneous. Or response patterns may differ as you move from one end of the table to the other. Whatever the case, it is important to examine data, such as that found in a table, from several angles. Similarly, variables having quantitative (ratio and interval) scales should be plotted as they are in the text. (Graphing software is so widely available that this shouldn't be a chore.) From such graphics you can determine the form of relationships and their strength and locate "outlying" observations, among other things.

■ **As we noted, assessing importance is one of the hardest tasks facing data analysts.** This problem has both statistical and substantive aspects, and both have to be considered simultaneously. Terms such as *statistical significance* and *explained variation* pertain to observed data, not to people's feelings and behavior. Therefore, finding that a chi-square is statistically significant may or may not be important. By the same token, the fact that income "explains 60 percent of the variation in political ideology" doesn't necessarily mean we know much about why people are liberals, moderates, or conservatives. Data analysis helps us understand, but it does not replace hard thought about the substance of a topic.

Here is an example that may tie these ideas together. An investigator wants to know if Americans are more knowledgeable about government and politics than Germans. She conducts a survey of 5,000 citizens in each country (total $N = 10,000$) and discovers that 20 percent of Americans and 25 percent of Germans can name their representatives to the local legislature. Statistically speaking, this would be a highly significant difference. But does it have practical importance? Most observers would probably say, "No, there's no functional or meaningful difference. The statistical significance is a product of the huge sample size."

Exercise 13–1. Chapter 13 in the text discusses the analysis of two variables. One of the first topics discussed was cross-tabulation. Answer each of the following questions about why and how we might use a cross-tabulation for analysis.

a. Cross-tabulations are for categorical data. What is categorical data?

_____

_____

b. Why would it be difficult—if not impossible—to use a cross-tabulation to examine two variables that capture continuous data rather than categorical data?

_____

_____

c. The text states that "when the categories of the independent variable are arrayed across the *top* of the table—that is, they are the column labels—it is essential that the percentages add to 100 down the columns. These are called *column percentages*." Why must the column percentages equal 100?

_____

_____

d. For what purpose would you use gamma in analyzing data in a cross-tabulation?

_____

_____

e. How would you interpret a gamma value of 1? How would you interpret a gamma value of -1?

_____

_____

f. How much magnitude (the distance from 0) would you want to see in gamma before concluding that there is a strong relationship between the variables?

_____

_____

Exercise 13–2. Statisticians frequently use graphs to visualize relationships. Look at figure 13–1. It displays what we have labeled a strong "negative linear correlation" between Y and X.

FIGURE 13–1

Example of Negative Linear Correlation

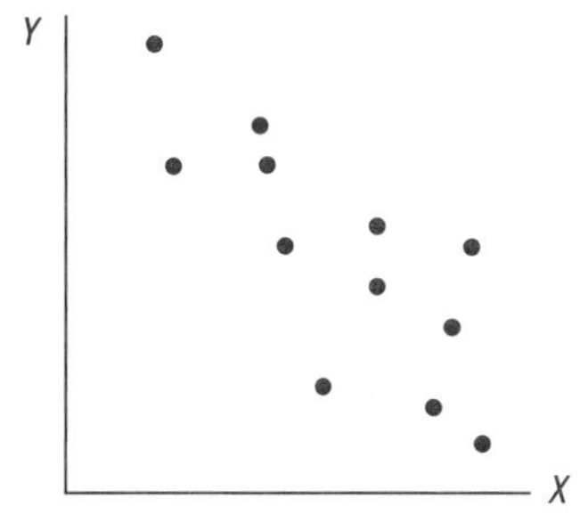

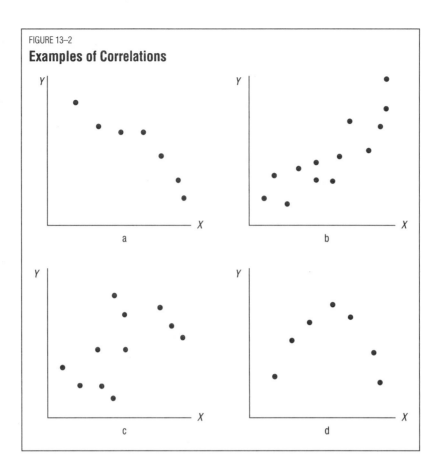

FIGURE 13–2

Examples of Correlations

Describe the type and (approximate) strength of the four relationships shown in figure 13–2.

a. _____

_____

b. _____

_____

c. _____

_____

d. _____

_____

TABLE 13–1

Data on Ethnicity and Voting

Ethnicity	Turnout	N
White	Voted	150
White	Did not vote	50
Nonwhite	Voted	30
Nonwhite	Did not vote	20

Exercise 13–3. Using the hypothetical data given in table 13–1, create a contingency table to examine the relationship between ethnicity and political participation, as measured by voting. Make sure that you include the appropriate percentages as well as the frequencies.

a. Attach your table.

b. In your opinion, does a relationship exist between voting and ethnicity? Briefly explain.

_____

_____

_____

_____

_____

c. Thinking of percentages in probability terms, what is the *probability* of a nonwhite person voting? _____ Of a white person voting? _____

d. What are the *odds* of a white person voting as opposed to not voting? _____ The odds of a nonwhite person voting as opposed to not voting? _____

e. What is the odds ratio? _____ Briefly interpret this number.

_____

_____

_____

_____

_____

Exercise 13–4. Table 13–2 is a contingency table from a computer program that shows the relationship between region and the political parties of ninety-nine US senators. (One independent senator is not included.)

TABLE 13–2

Cross-Tabulation of Senators' Party Identification and Region

Party Identification	Region				Total
	1	2	3	4	
1 Democrat	16	9	14	10	49
% within region	69.6%	37.5%	53.8%	38.5%	49.5%
2 Republican	7	15	12	16	50
% within region	30.4%	62.5%	46.2%	61.5%	50.5%
Total	23	24	26	26	99
% within region	100.0%	100.0%	100.0%	100.0%	100%

Source: Computer-generated table.

a. Do the data indicate that Democratic and Republican senators tend to come from different regions of the country?

_____

_____

b. If you did not know which region a senator was from, what would be your best guess of his or her party affiliation?

_____

_____

c. What would be an appropriate measure of association? Why?

_____

_____

_____

d. Calculate the measure that you identified in part c.

_____

_____

_____

Exercise 13–5.   Examine the data presented in table 13–3.

TABLE 13–3
Cross-Tabulation of Prayer by Political Ideology

| | Political Orientation | | | |
| | 1 | 2 | 3 | |
PRAY: How often does R pray	Liberal	Moderate	Conservative	Total
1 Several times a day	33	71	91	195
	18.0%	23.9%	41.7%	27.9%
2 Once a day	53	86	64	203
	29.0%	29.0%	29.4%	29.1%
3 Several times a week	22	48	25	95
	12.0%	16.2%	11.5%	13.6%
4 Once a week	17	18	14	49
	9.3%	6.1%	6.4%	7.0%
5 Less than once a week	55	72	23	150
	30.1%	24.2%	10.6%	21.5%
6 Never	3	2	1	6
	1.6%	.7%	.5%	.9%
Total	183	297	218	698
	100.0%	100.0%	100.0%	100.0%

Source: Computer-generated table.

a. Which is the independent variable? Which is the dependent variable? Describe the relationship between the variables.

_____

_____

_____

_____

_____

_____

b. The gamma value for the data in the table is –.288. What does gamma tell you about the relationship between political orientation and frequency of praying? Why does gamma have a negative sign?

_____

_____

_____

_____

_____

_____

Exercise 13–6. In this exercise you will analyze data using a chi-square test. Use the hypothetical data in table 13-3 to assess whether the variables are statistically independent. Remember that the chi-square statistic is not a very good indicator of the strength of an association. If this were a full analysis of the data, you might measure strength through an analysis of percentages. Here we are simply using chi-square to test for statistical significance. Use a one-tailed test and $\alpha = .05$.

TABLE 13–3

Relationship between X and Y Based on Sample of 200

Variable Y	Variable X		
	A	B	TOTAL
A	20	30	50
B	23	35	58
C	57	35	92
Total	100	100	200

a. What is the observed chi-square value?

_____

b. How many degrees of freedom do you have?

_____

117

c. What is the critical chi-square value?

_____

d. Are variables X and Y statistically independent? Why or why not?

_____

Exercise 13–7. A major and continuing controversy in American politics has been the privatizing of governmental functions. Some states, for example, have turned to private contractors to house and rehabilitate their prisoners. Advocates claim that this practice saves the taxpayers money. Critics, however, say that these institutions, which are run on a for-profit basis, cut corners in inmate care and supervision.

TABLE 13–4

Inmate Deaths by Facility

Type of Facility	Mean	Number of Institutions
Federal	8.86	(112)
State	19.48	(1,225)
Private	4.65	(110)
Total	17.53	(1,447)

Source	Sum of Squares	Degrees of Freedom	Mean Square	Observed F	Probability
Explained (type of prison)	31,341.430	2	15,670.715	7.490	.0006
Error	3,020,990.558	1,444	2,092.099		
Total	3,052,331.988	1,446			

Your employer, a nonprofit criminal justice organization, has funded a study of the issue. A small part of the resulting data appears in table 13–4. Your boss asks you to make sense of these numbers. This portion of the analysis involves two variables collected by the Bureau of Justice Statistics: (1) the operator of the facility, a federal or state agency or a private corporation, and (2) answers to the following question asked of supervisors: "Between July 1, 1994, and June 30, 1995, how many total inmates died while under the jurisdiction of this facility?"

a. What type of analysis is this? Regression, analysis of variance, or what?

_____

b. What is the objective of this analysis?

_____

_____

c. Did type of the facility (federal, state, private) have an effect on death rates among inmates? Explain.

_____

_____

d. Look at the data in both tables. Can you translate the problem into a statistical hypothesis? Explain it to your employer.

_____

_____

e. Assuming these data came from a random sample of prisons in the United States (they did not), could the differences between the death rates be attributable to sampling error, or is there evidence that the type of operator has an effect on mortality? Explain your answer. (*Hint:* This is a question of statistics, not substance.)

_____

_____

f. Interpret these data and statistical results substantively—that is, in a way that makes sense to journalists and public officials. Try to think of a reason why the statistical results reported in item 13–7e came out as they did. Are we observing a direct connection between type of prison and inmate death rates, or are there other variables that ought to be taken into account? Does the study shed any light on the policy debate about privatization?

_____

_____

_____

_____

Exercise 13–8. Open the "Social Vote" file available on the PSRM Web site using the statistical package recommended by your instructor. For this exercise you will use the variables *pia11e* and *party*. Note that *pia11e* measures whether the respondent encouraged anyone to vote for Barack Obama or Mitt Romney by posting on a social networking site, such as Facebook or Twitter, in the last thirty days. *Party* measures whether the respondent leans toward the Republican or Democratic Party or neither. The first step is to select only the cases where *party* equals 1 (Republican), 2 (Democrat), or 3 (independent). Next, select only cases where *pia11e* equals 1 (yes) or 2 (no). This will leave you with 914 cases. Once you have prepared the data successfully, you are ready to answer the questions below.

a. Use your statistical package to create a cross-tabulation using the selected variables and to calculate chi-square. Attach the table you generate.

b. Using the cross-tabulation you generated, calculate chi-square by hand. The result should match the answer from your statistical package. Show your work below.

Exercise 13–9. Do political party leaders represent their rank-and-file members? Do their opinions and stands on issues generally agree with those of their supporters, or are they more liberal or conservative? Richard Herrera investigated this question by comparing the mean views of delegates to the 1988 Democratic Party convention, presumably a good cross-section of party leaders, with those of Democratic voters.[1] He hypothesized that if leaders are out of touch with followers, there will be a difference between their average issue positions. A small portion of his results can be seen in table 13–5.

TABLE 13–5
Mean Views of Democratic Delegates and Democratic Voters, 1988

Issue	Mean Delegate View	Mean Partisan Voter View	Mean Difference and Significance
Defense spending	2.33	3.11	−.78**
Get along with Russia	2.24	3.23	−.99**
Government helps blacks	2.86	1.92	−.94**
Place of women	1.47	2.46	−.99**

Source: Richard Herrera, "Are 'Superdelegates' Super?," *Political Behavior* 16 (March 1994): 88.

** = Significant at .01 level.

The mean delegate and partisan voter responses are given on seven-point scales. For instance, both delegates and a random sample of Democratic voters were asked about their opinions on defense spending. A 1 on the scale represents the most liberal position (that is, we should cut defense spending), whereas 7 is the most conservative stance. If everyone in a particular group were liberal, the mean score would be 1. The other questions, for which respondents could reply on similar seven-point scales, were as follows: "Should we try to get along with Russia?" (1), or is this a "big mistake?" (7); "Should the government in Washington make every effort to improve the social and economic position of blacks?" (1), or should there be "no special effort?" (7); and "Should women have an equal role with men in running business, industry, or government?" (1), or is a woman's place "in the home?" (7). The last column represents the difference in

---

[1] Richard Herrera, "Are 'Superdelegates' Super?," *Political Behavior* 16 (March 1994): 79–92.

means between delegates and voters. The author writes that the symbol ** means "difference is significant at p .01."[2] Try to make sense of these results.

a. What general hypothesis is the author investigating?

b. What statistical hypothesis does each line of the table test?

c. Which of these statistical hypotheses should Herrera reject and why?

d. So far you have considered statistical hypotheses. Should they be rejected or not? Now translate these results into terms an average citizen can understand. What, in short, do the results say about Democratic leaders and average party voters? (*Hint:* Always keep in mind the meaning of the questions and the scales. In other words, if one person has a higher score than another individual on, say, the defense spending issue, would you say the first person was more liberal or conservative than the second?)

Exercise 13–10. In this exercise you will use an F-test to test a hypothesis that population means are equal using the data in table 13–6. This table reports the number of political yard signs placed in yards by Democrats, Republicans, and independents. In this exercise we want to test the null hypothesis that the population means are equal using an F-test. Answer the questions below. (*Hint:* you can refer to the "How It's Done" box in the text as a guide for how to calculate sums of squares.)

TABLE 13-6

Number of Political Yard Signs Planted by Party ID

Number of Political Yard Signs (X)

Democrats	Republicans	Independents
0	0	0
2	0	0
3	4	1
5	6	3
7	9	4

a. Calculate the between, within, and total degrees of freedom. Label each.

b. Calculate the between sum of squares.

c. Calculate the within sum of squares.

d. Calculate the total sum of squares.

e. Calculate F.

f. Find the F critical score in appendix D in the text for a 95 percent confidence level (alpha = .05).

g. Are the population means statistically significantly different? How do you know?

Exercise 13–11. In this exercise you will use the "Human Development" data set available on the PSRM Web site to test the relationship between life expectancy and education. Open the data file in the statistical package identified by your instructor. You will test the relationship between the variables *life_expectancy* and *mean_years_schooling* in a bivariate regression to answer the questions below.

a. Write a testable hypothesis about the relationship between life expectancy and education. Make sure to include both a null and alternative hypothesis.

b. Enter the variables in your statistical package and run an ordinary least squares regression. Attach the output to this exercise.

_____

c. Interpret the coefficient (the slope) in the context of your hypothesis.

_____

d. Decide whether you accept the null or alternative hypothesis with consideration of both substantive and statistical significance using a two-tailed test with 95 percent confidence.

_____

_____

e. Which statistics did you use to make your conclusion in item d? How did you determine statistical significance?

_____

_____

Exercise 13–12. At the heart of a regression analysis is the concept of minimizing the squared errors. Using figures 13-14 and 13-15 in the textbook and the associated discussion, answer the following questions.

a. Explain in plain English how a regression minimizes the squared errors. Why does a regression give us a single line that best fits the data?

_____

_____

_____

_____

b. What is the difference between an observed value of Y and a predicted value of Y?

_____

_____

_____

_____

c. Why would one expect to see all of the data points on the line representing the mean and the regression line if an independent variable perfectly predicts a dependent variable?

_____

_____

_____

_____

Exercise 13–13. The following hypothetical data can be used to analyze political communication among friends. In this example we try to assess how Facebook friends communicate political information. We have data on the number of times each Facebook user was exposed to political information from a friend and how many times that user shared political information with a friend. We suspect that an increase in exposure to political information causes an increase in the sharing of political information.

Use the data in table 13–7, where *exposure to political info* is the independent variable and *political info shared with another* is the dependent variable, to plot the regression line. Remember that in order to plot a regression line you will first need to perform all of the underlying calculations to find *b, a,* and predicted values of *Y.*

TABLE 13–7

Exposure to and Sharing of Political Information

i	Exposure to Political Info	Political Info Shared with Another
1	2	2
2	1	3
3	1	1
4	5	8
5	4	3
6	7	5
7	7	7
8	2	1
9	3	6
10	0	0

Exercise 13–14. Define each of the following and explain how you would use each in an analysis of a bivariate relationship.

- R^2
- r
- Y
- Y_i
- a
- b
- e

Exercise 13–15. In this exercise you will use a regression to predict the vote percentage for Barack Obama in each state in the 2012 presidential election. To do this you will use the "States" data file available on the PSRM Web site. You will be testing the hypothesis that more voters identifying as conservative in a state led to a higher percentage of votes for Mitt Romney. To test the relationship you should use the *conservative* and *romneyvotepercent2012* variables in an ordinary least squares regression in the statistical package your instructor has chosen. Answer the questions below.

a. Prepare a scatter plot of the percentage of votes for Romney (*Y*) against the number of conservative voters. Attach it to the assignment. Can you discern a relationship?

_____

_____

b. Compute Pearson's r, the correlation coefficient? What does it tell you about conservative voters and the percentage vote for Romney?

_____

_____

c. Use the statistical package to run an ordinary least squares regression with *conservative* as the independent variable and *vote percentage for Romney* as the dependent variable. What is the estimated regression equation?

_____

_____

d. Interpret the regression coefficient statistically and substantively.

_____

_____

e. Is the regression coefficient statistically significant? At what level? Explain.

_____

_____

Exercise 13–16. Suppose a political scientist hypothesizes that lower economic growth rates will be associated with greater political instability. His thinking rests on this logic: In a world of satellite television, the Internet, and video cell phones, people increasingly expect and demand the living standards they see in developed nations. If national productivity does not bring these rewards, citizens become frustrated and place heavy demands on the political system. Instability, even violence, may result. If, on the other hand, the economy can meet demands for higher living standards, government will have greater legitimacy. To test this idea the researcher collects data for a sample of thirty-four nations. The dependent variable, a measure of political stability, is a percentile that ranges from 0 to 100, with 0 meaning the least stability and 100 the most. The independent variable is the percentage per capita growth rate in gross domestic product (GDP) in 2005.[3] The investigator, who is writing an article for publication, claims that these data support his proposition, but he asks for your opinion before sending the paper to a journal. Answer the questions below and render an opinion.

Table 13–8 presents the results of a regression analysis of political stability on GDP growth in a format that commonly appears in scholarly journals. Not much information seems to be supplied. But in fact you can reconstruct the significance tests. Assume that the null hypotheses pertaining to the regression parameters equal zero. (As we say in the text, these are the usual null hypotheses.) Note that the standard errors appear in parentheses below the estimated coefficients. Hence, you can compute the observed t values. Similarly, the degrees of freedom and the critical t (for any level of significance listed in appendix B in the text) can be determined because you have the sample size.

TABLE 13–8

Regression Analysis of Political Stability on GDP Growth

	Estimated Constant and Coefficient (standard error)
Constant	79.31**
	(12.36)
Growth in GDP	−6.569*
	(2.707)

Source: CIA World Fact Book, 2007.

$N = 34$, $R^2 = .155$.

*Significant at .05. **Significant at .001.

---

[3] GDP data are from the *CIA World Fact Book*, https://www.cia.gov/cia/publications/factbook/fields/ 2003.html.

a. Compute the observed *t* for the regression constant.

_____

_____

b. Compute the observed *t* for the regression coefficient.

_____

_____

c. What are the degrees of freedom for testing the significance of the regression coefficient?

_____

_____

d. What is the critical *t* at the .05 level for a two-tailed test?

_____

_____

e. The asterisk in the table suggests that $\hat{b} = -6.569$ is statistically significant. Is this assertion correct? Why or why not?

_____

_____

f. What proportion of the variation in political stability is "explained" by growth in GDP?

_____

_____

g. What is the correlation coefficient (*r*) between stability and growth? (*Hint:* What is the connection between R^2 and *r*?)

_____

_____

h. In sum, do the data support the political scientist's research hypothesis (not the null or alternative hypothesis) about the effect of economic change on political stability? Explain your answer. (*Hint:* Look carefully at the regression coefficient and think about what the number means in substantive or practical terms.)

_____

_____

_____

_____

Exercise 13–17.   For this exercise you will use a difference of means test to test the hypothesis that older citizens hold the Supreme Court in higher regard than do younger citizens. The data include two random samples drawn independently, and you should assume the variances are equal. Sample 1 includes thirty citizens thirty years of age or older with a sample mean of 87 and a population standard deviation of 4. Sample 2 includes twenty-five citizens under age thirty with a sample mean of 85 and a population standard deviation of 3. Choose a confidence level with which you are comfortable and explain why you chose that level. Then decide if you accept the hypothesis. (*Hint:* Remember that the variance is the square of the standard deviation.)

_____

_____

_____

_____

_____

_____

_____

CHAPTER 14

Multivariate Analysis

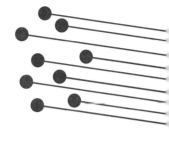

In chapter 14 we present several different statistical methods, or models, for investigating relationships that involve a dependent variable and more than a single independent variable. Multivariate analysis helps researchers to discover spurious relationships, to measure the effect of changes in multiple independent variables on a dependent variable, and, generally, to strengthen claims about causal relationships. Multivariate statistical procedures allow researchers to control statistically for other factors instead of controlling other factors experimentally. Substitution of statistical control for experimental control is not a perfect solution in the quest to establish causal explanations for political phenomena, and, therefore, results and claims based on statistical evidence must be scrutinized carefully.

As with bivariate data analysis, the choice of analytical procedure depends on the way variables, particularly the dependent variable, are measured:

- Contingency table analysis is used when the data are categorical—that is, when the variables have categories. This method quickly becomes unwieldy and difficult to interpret as the number of tables and cells increases and the number of cases or observations in cells decreases.

- Linear multiple regression investigates whether there is a linear relationship between a numerically measured dependent variable and multiple independent variables and allows researchers to assess how much a one-unit change in an independent variable changes the dependent variable when all the other variables have been taken into account or controlled. So-called dummy variables are used when there are categorical independent variables.

- A logistic regression model is used when the dependent variable is dichotomous (that is, a binary variable with values of 0 or 1) and estimates the probability that the dependent variable equals 1 as a linear function of the independent variables.

Also, as with bivariate data analysis, we are interested in the strength of the relationship, or how well the model fits the data, and in the statistical significance of our findings.

Although some models and statistical procedures can get quite complicated, with practice you will be able to use at least the simpler ones and to interpret their results. The exercises in this chapter give you practice in deciding which procedure is appropriate to use, how to relate your data to the procedure, and how to interpret the results of the analyses.

Exercise 14–1. Here are a few questions to spark your curiosity. Below are descriptions of possible causal relationships. For each one identify the causal assertion and draw an arrow diagram similar to the ones used in chapters 13 and 14 of the textbook to represent it. Then, think of a third variable (or variables) that might explain the original relationship. Draw another arrow diagram to illustrate the possible three-variable association. Here is an example. Suppose someone tells you, "There is a statistically significant relationship between foot size and the number of words in the vocabularies of the students in the Denver, Colorado, public school system. Children with big feet tend to know many more words than children with dainty feet."[1] This statement asserts a relationship between foot size and size of vocabulary. If the relationship were causal, it could be diagrammed, as shown in figure 14–1.

FIGURE 14–1

X
(foot size) ⟶ Y
(number of words in vocabulary)

It is of course not clear that the size of anyone's feet causes vocabulary acquisition. Instead, the relationship probably reflects aging: as children get older, their feet grow larger *and* they develop larger vocabularies (figure 14–2).

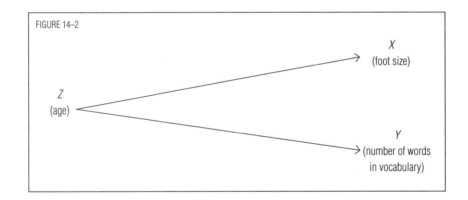

FIGURE 14–2

Z
(age)

X
(foot size)

Y
(number of words in vocabulary)

The key to answering these questions is to think and reason carefully.

a. "Should violence on cable television be more closely regulated by government? The *Washington Post* reports that the Federal Communications Commission found that 'a *correlation* exists between bloodshed on television and violence in real life.'"[2] Think of a factor that might explain the relationship and draw the two diagrams. Briefly discuss your ideas.

_____

_____

_____

_____

---

[1] Stimulated by an example at "Spurious Correlation and Its Detection," *Autobox.com*, http://www.autobox.com/spur10.html.

[2] John Dunbar, "FCC: Govt. Could Regulate TV Violence," *Washington Post*, April 25, 2007, http://www.washingtonpost.com/wp-dyn/content/article/2007/04/25/AR2007042502332.html.

b. *Claim:* There is a strong and statistically significant positive correlation between the percentage of Hispanics in a city and the percentage of students who do not complete high school. What is the causal assertion, and what is a possible alternative?

c. "The [Dartmouth Medical School] team found a direct correlation between the number of smoking scenes watched and the chances of becoming a habitual smoker: Children who had seen the most scenes were twice as likely to end up addicted as those who had seen the fewest.... The study is in the September issue of the *Archives of Pediatrics and Adolescent Medicine.*"[3] What is the causal claim? Can you think of an alternative explanation? Illustrate your discussion with diagrams.

d. Senator Sam Brownback, Republican, said in a televised debate on September 5, 2007, "In countries that have redefined marriage, where they've said, 'Okay, it's not just a man and a woman, it can be two men, two women,' the marriage rates in those countries have plummeted to where you have countries now in northern Europe where 80 percent of the firstborn children are born out of wedlock.... And currently in this country—currently—we're at 36 percent of our children born out of wedlock."[4] What claim is Senator Brownback making? There may be several, but just pick one—try to recast it as a causal assertion and think of a possible alternative explanation for the relationship he asserts.

e. An article on the Web site of the Heritage Foundation, a Washington, D.C., policy organization (think tank), asserts, "Many lawmakers in Congress and in the states assume that the high level of crime in America must have its roots in material conditions, such as poor employment opportunities and a shortage of adequately funded social programs.... The central proposition in official Washington's thinking about crime is that poverty is the primary cause of crime." The author of the article disagrees with this statement and argues instead that the number one cause of the development of criminal behavior is fatherless families. He writes, "Over the past thirty years, the rise in violent crime parallels the rise in families abandoned by fathers.... High-crime neighborhoods are characterized by high concentrations of families abandoned by fathers.... State-by-state analysis by Heritage scholars indicates that a 10 percent increase in the percentage of children living in single-parent homes leads typically to a 17 percent increase in juvenile crime.... The rate of violent teenage crime corresponds with the number of families abandoned by fathers."[5] Here you have an implicit debate between "many lawmakers" and researchers at the Heritage

[3] Rick Weiss, "Science Notebook," *WashingtonPost.com,* September 24, 2007, http://www.washingtonpost.com/wp-dyn/content/article/2007/09/23/AR2007092300770.html.

[4] "The Claim," *WashingtonPost.com,* September 19, 2007, http://www.washingtonpost.com/wp-dyn/content/article/2007/09/18/AR2007091801864.html.

[5] Patrick F. Fagan, "The Real Root Causes of Violent Crime: The Breakdown of Marriage, Family, and Community," *The Heritage Foundation,* March 17, 1995, http://www.heritage.org/Research/Crime/BG1026.cfm.

Foundation and elsewhere. Use arrow diagrams to illustrate their causal arguments. Then try to think of a way of reconciling these positions. Is it possible, in other words, that both sides are partly correct? Again use diagrams to help clarify your thinking.

_____

_____

_____

Exercise 14–2. Here are a few research hypotheses and designs. For each explain what would be an appropriate tool for statistical analysis and why. (*Hint:* What are the dependent and independent variables and how are they measured?)

a. An investigator believes acts of terrorism are caused mainly by sudden decreases in the economic standard of living of large numbers of society members.[6] Data collected from fifty-five nations consist of the occurrence of an act of terror in a given year (yes or no) and measures of changes in income, poverty, employment, and manufacturing and agricultural output for the previous year.

_____

_____

_____

_____

b. A social scientist wonders whether the Sunbelt states are as politically conservative as they are reputed to be. She believes that, apart from perhaps social issues, the opinions and beliefs of people in different regions are roughly the same. Moreover, she thinks that any variation among regions stems mainly from differences in the social class composition of the citizens living in those places. Her data are in the American National Election Study 2000 data file that has categorical measures of region, attitudes on economic issues, and demographic characteristics, such as income, education, and ethnicity.[7] What would be a good way to explore this hypothesis with these data?

_____

_____

_____

_____

_____

_____

_____

---

[6] Incidentally, for a classic statement of this hypothesis see Crane Brinton, *The Anatomy of Revolution,* rev. and exp. ed. (Englewood Cliffs, N.J.: Prentice Hall, 1965).

[7] This topic would make a great research project for a student with access to the American National Election Study data and statistical software.

c. A Washington think tank wants to know why some states have more generous health care benefits for the poor than others. It hypothesizes that two general factors explain the difference: states' overall political philosophy (degree of liberalism, for example) and economic capacity. The more liberal and wealthy a state, the more generous its health programs. The group's research firm has numerical indicators of health spending per capita for the poor, ideology,[8] percentage voting Democratic in national and state elections for the past ten years, per capita income, and economic growth over the past year. What method do you suggest the think tank use to test its hypothesis?

_____

_____

_____

_____

_____

d. A student in a political communications class wants to know if a newspaper's size, as measured by average weekly circulation, affected its coverage of the 2004 National Democratic Convention, as indicated by the average number of column inches it devoted to the subject in the month of July. He has spent considerable time collecting these data for forty papers throughout the United States. But he wonders whether coverage will also be influenced by the papers' political partisanship and region, for which he has only indicator or categorical variables. (Party bias, for instance, is coded into three categories—"pro-Democratic," "neutral," and "pro-Republican"—whereas region is indexed simply as 0 for "non-South" and 1 for "South.") Can you help this student pick an appropriate statistical strategy for investigating the hypothesis? How would your strategy handle the independent variables?

_____

_____

_____

_____

_____

_____

_____

_____

Exercise 14–3. Multivariate analysis simply means the simultaneous examination of three or more variables. With categorical data, researchers _can_ analyze contingency tables. Empirical social science has in practice, however, largely gone beyond this type of analysis, but the examination of multi-way contingency tables provides an excellent introduction to more advanced methods. The general idea is easily grasped. It consists of three steps:

---

[8] Measures of states' ideology exist and are widely used. See, for example, Gerald C. Wright, Robert S. Erikson, and John P. McIver, "Measuring State Partisanship and Ideology with Survey Data," _Journal of Politics_ 47 (1985): 469–89. Also see William D. Berry, Evan J. Rinquist, Richard C. Fording, and Russell L. Hanson, "Measuring Citizen and Government Ideology in the American States, 1960–93," _American Journal of Political Science_ 42 (1998): 327–48.

1. Examine the relationship between the independent and dependent variables in a bivariate or two-way table. Ask yourself, how strong is the relationship? How are the individual categories related? (For example, you might find in a study of opinions on the environment that level of education is related to concerns about global warming: high school graduates are more concerned about global warming than are those individuals with less education by twenty-two percentage points.) Call this the *original relationship*. (Table 14–1 gives a new example.)

TABLE 14–1

Original Relationship: Voter by Gender

Vote in 2004	Male	Female
Kerry	46.4%	53.2%
Bush	53.6	46.8
Total	100%	100%
	(377)	(408)

Chi-square: 3.589; gamma: −.135; tau-*b*: −.068

Source: 2004 American National Election Study.

---

2. Analyze the two variables within each stratum of a control variable. That is, you will have a two-way table for each level of the control variable. Construct a multi-way table, as illustrated in table 14–2. Call this complex table the *controlled relationship*.

TABLE 14–2

Partial Relationships: Vote by Gender by Party

Vote	A. Democrats		B. Independents		C. Republicans	
	Male	Female	Male	Female	Male	Female
Kerry	89.9%	91.5%	55.6%	64.3%	8.5%	7.3%
Bush	10.1	8.5	44.4	35.7	91.5	92.7
Total	100%	100%	100%	100%	100%	100%
	(158)	(212)	(27)	(14)	(188)	(177)

Chi-square:.290; gamma: −.097; tau-*b* : −.028

Chi-square:.290; gamma: −.180; tau-*b* : −.084

Chi-square:.169; gamma:.080; tau-*b* :.022

---

3. Draw a conclusion. If the original relationship remains more or less the same in each level of the control variable, then the control variable does not have an impact; however, if the original relationship is weaker (or disappears) in most of the subtables, you have reason to suspect a spurious association. Or, if the relationship is not spurious, the control variable at least affects it statistically. It is also possible that the *Y-X* association will be even stronger in one or more of the subtables, a situation called *interaction*.

Here are some exercises to help you grasp the meaning of these ideas. The emphasis here is on conceptual understanding, not computation. Use table 14–2 showing vote by gender by party.

a. Is there a relationship between vote and gender? Explain. (*Hint:* Pay attention to the percentages, the measures of association, and the chi-square.)

_____

_____

_____

_____

b. The chi-square for this table is _____

What are the degrees of freedom? _____

Is there a statistically significant relationship at the .05 level? _____

We now introduce a control variable, party identification, which has three levels or categories: Democrat, independent, and Republican. Thus, there are three two-way tables, one for each category of party identification (table 14–2). Examine each table individually.

c. In subtable A (Democrats) is there a relationship between gender and vote? How strong is it? Is the chi-square significant at the .05 level? Explain.

_____

_____

_____

d. Give a similar analysis for subtable B (independents). Describe the relationship, if any.

_____

_____

_____

e. What is the relationship between vote and gender among Republicans (subtable C)?

_____

_____

_____

TABLE 14–3

Death Penalty by Defendant's Race

| Death Penalty? | Defendant's Race | |
	White	Black
Yes	19	17
No	141	149

Exercise 14–4. A speaker at a lecture declares that no statistical evidence whatsoever demonstrates that the death penalty discriminates against minorities. When pressed on the point, she shows a slide that looks like table 14–3.[9] The subjects were 326 defendants indicted for murder in Florida during 1976 and 1977.

[9] These are "real" data first presented by M. Radlet, "Racial Characteristics and the Imposition of the Death Penalty," *American Sociological Review* 46 (1981): 918–27, cited in Alan Agresti, *Analysis of Ordinal Categorical Data* (New York: Wiley, 1984), 6.

a. Do these data show a relationship between race and receiving the death penalty? Explain your answer in words and with a table and an appropriate test statistic.

_____

_____

_____

_____

_____

_____

_____

Now suppose another panelist says, "Wait a minute! These data tell only part of the story. If they are broken down by the race of the *victim* as well, we see that there is discrimination." He presents the data shown in table 14–4.[10]

TABLE 14–4

Death Penalty by Victim and Defendant's Race

| | Victim's Race (Z) | | | |
| | White Defendant's Race (X) | | Black Defendant's Race (X) | |
Death Penalty? (Y)	White	Black	White	Black
Yes	19	11	0	6
No	132	52	9	97
Total	151	63	9	103

b. Can you interpret table 14–4? What, if anything, does it say about the discriminatory effects of the application of the death penalty in Florida during that time? (*Hint:* Look at the subtables one at a time and calculate percentages.)

_____

_____

_____

_____

_____

_____

_____

[10] Agresti, *Analysis of Ordinal Categorical Data,* 32.

HELPFUL HINTS

Interpreting Regression Results

Here's a useful trick for understanding both the statistical and the substantive meaning of the coefficients of regression analysis. First, keep in mind the meaning of a multiple regression coefficient: it measures the amount Y changes for a one-unit change in a particular independent variable when all other independent variables have been held constant. This somewhat abstract definition can be made more meaningful when reading research results by following these steps:

1. Examine the summary table. For example, suppose, as is commonly the case, the findings are presented in a table like this.

Effects of Education and Race on Trust in the Judicial System

Variable	Coefficient
Constant	20***
Education (in years), X_1	2.0**
Race (0 for white, 1 for nonwhite), X_2	−3.0**
$R^2 = .45$; ***$p < .001$, **$p < .01$.	

Here the dependent variable (Y) is a scale of trust in the judicial system; the higher the score, the greater the trust. There are two independent variables, education and race, with the latter coded as a dummy variable (0 for whites, 1 for nonwhites).

2. Write the regression coefficients, including the constant if there is one, as an equation. Place the numeric values of the coefficients in an equation.

$$\widehat{Y} = 20 + 2.0\text{Educ} - 3.0\text{Race}.$$

Notice that we have included the constant term (20) and a minus sign before the coefficient for race. It is essential to keep track of the signs of the coefficients.

3. Imagine that the value of all independent variables is 0. Substitute this value into the equation. Example:

$$\widehat{Y} = 20 + 2.0(0) - 3.0(0) = 20.$$

What does this mean? If a person had no schooling (0 years) and was white ($X_2 = 0$), the predicted level of trust ($\widehat{Y}$) would be 20 units.

4. Now imagine that a person with no education ($X_1 = 0$) becomes nonwhite. Notice X_1 stays constant (that is, education is the same as in the previous equation) and only X_2 changes, from 0 to 1. Place these new values in the equation and simplify.

$$\widehat{Y} = 20 + 2.0(0) - 3.0(1) = 20 - 3.0 = 17.$$

This result clearly demonstrates that race—when education is held constant—"causes" or is associated with a three-unit decrease in trust of the judicial system.

5. Now make another substitution. Go back to whites ($X_2 = 0$) and assume education increases by one year.

$$\widehat{Y} = 20 + 2.0(1) - 3.0(0) = 20 + 2.0 = 22.$$

We see that an additional year of education increases trust among whites by two units.

6. Make additional substitutions until you have a feel for the impact of the variables. Suppose, for instance, a nonwhite individual has twelve years of education. What is her predicted trust score?

$$\widehat{Y} = 20 + 2.0(12) - 3.0(1) = 20 + 24.0 - 3.0 = 41.$$

7. After making these kinds of changes, you should be able to write a substantive summary of the regression model. In this case it appears that as people acquire more education, they have more trust in the court system. This is true of both whites and nonwhites. But for a given level of education, trust among nonwhites is lower than among whites. Your next step would be to expand on this conclusion. You might hypothesize that both poorly educated people and members of minority groups have different experiences in the criminal justice system. Of course, that argument goes beyond the data presented here.

(Continued)

137

(Continued)

8. The estimated coefficients are the heart and soul of the research. The information at the bottom of the table—this format is typical of published articles—shows how well the data fit the linear regression model. The multiple regression coefficient, R^2, indicates that about half of the observed variation in trust scores is "explained" by education and race. The asterisks beside the coefficients indicate the level of significance. All three estimates are statistically significant, one at the .001 level, the others at the .01 level. (It is common for the coefficients in a model to have different degrees of significance.)

Exercise 14–5. Assume that two factors explain the number of representatives in national assemblies: population size and geographic size. Use the following regression coefficient values in table 14–5 to answer the question below. Population is measured in millions and geographic size is measured in square miles.

TABLE 14-5

Variable	Coefficient
Constant	100*
Population (in millions), X_1	.5*
Geographic size (in millions of square miles), X_2	42*
*$p < .01$	

In which of the following countries would assembly membership be predicted to be highest? Why? (*Hint:* Use the least squares equation to predict assembly membership.) What are the predicted values for each country?

Country 1: population = 300; geographic size = 1.8

Country 2: population = 85; geographic size = 0.6

_____

_____

_____

_____

_____

_____

Exercise 14–6. Table 14–6 contains the results of a multiple regression analysis of the effects of development status (X_1), GNP (X_2), and infant mortality rates (deaths per 1,000 live births; X_3) on an indicator of political freedom, voice, and accountability (Y). The status variable is an indicator, or dummy variable, that is coded 0 for developed nations and 1 for developing nations. The dependent variable measures "the extent to which a country's citizens are able to participate in selecting their government, as well as freedom of expression, freedom of association, and free media. The index is scaled so that the mean of all scores is 0 and the standard deviation is 1.0. The higher the score, the greater the freedom."[11] The observed range goes from −1.870 to 1.450 or 3.32.

[11] Daniel Kaufmann, Aart Kraay, and Massimo Mastruzzi, "Aggregate and Individual Governance Indicators for 1996–2005," World Bank Policy Research Working Paper 4012, September 2006.

TABLE 14–6

Voice and Accountability Regressed on Development Status, GNP, and Infant Mortality

Variable	Coefficient (standard error)	Mean	Observed Minimum	Observed Maximum
Constant	.9533			
	(.3415)			
Status	−1.4558	.5278	0	1
	(.3270)			
GNP	.00000798	18450	600	68,800
	(.00000925)			
Infant mortality	−.00145	29.44	2	118
	(.002843)			

a. What is the estimated regression model?

b. Interpret the coefficient for status (X_1). Do not provide a mechanical answer, but try to explain in terms an informed nonstatistician can understand.

c. The coefficients in the table are called *partial coefficients*. Explain this term to a layperson. Use the estimated coefficient −1.4558 in the explanation.

Exercise 14–7. Political scientist Paul Goren investigated the relationship between core values and beliefs and policy preferences.[12] Goren defined *core beliefs* as "general descriptive beliefs about human nature and society in matters of public affairs," while *core values* are "evaluative standards citizens use to judge alternative social and political arrangements." He wanted to know if, how, and under what conditions these perceptions and attitudes affect opinions on public policy, such as governmental welfare programs. Table 14–7 contains a small portion of his research results.

---

[12] Paul Goren, "Core Principles and Policy Reasoning in Mass Publics: A Test of Two Theories," *British Journal of Political Science* 31 (January 2001): 159–77. The coefficients used in this assignment differ from those in the published table. The changes were made after personal communication with the author.

TABLE 14–7

Social Welfare Policy Opposition Regressed on Eight Independent Variables

Variable	Coefficient	(Standard Error)
Constant	11.99	(.98)
Race	−1.57	(.45)
Gender	−.76	(.30)
Family income quartile	.03	(.14)
Party identification	.43	(.14)
Feelings toward beneficiaries	−.03	(.00)
Economic individualism	.20	(.04)
Equal opportunity opposition	.58	(.06)
Political expertise	.03	(.07)

$R^2 = .48$; $F_{9,637}$; $df = 73.42$; $N = 638$

Source: Goren, "Core Principles and Policy Reasoning in Mass Publics," table 2.

The variables are as follows:

- Dependent variable, Y: Opposition to government social welfare provision. Additive, twenty-five-point scale for which higher scores indicate greater opposition to governmental welfare services and spending.
- Independent variables, X_k:

  - X_1: Race. 0 if white, 1 if African American.
  - X_2: Gender. 0 if male, 1 if female.
  - X_3: Income. Family income quartile (1–4).
  - X_4: Party identification. Seven-point scale: 0 for strong Democrat, 1 for Democrat, 2 for independent-leaning Democrat, 3 for independent, 4 for independent-leaning Republican, 5 for Republican, and 6 for strong Republican.
  - X_5: Feelings toward beneficiaries. Summation of thermometer scores of feelings toward blacks, poor people, and people on welfare. The higher the score, the warmer the feelings.
  - X_6: Economic individualism. Scale of belief that "hard work pays off." Twenty-five-point additive scale with high scores indicating that being industrious, responsible, and self-reliant leads to economic success.
  - X_7: Equal opportunity opposition. Belief "that society should do what is necessary to ensure that everyone has the same chance to get ahead in life." Thirteen-point additive scale with higher scores indicating increased opposition to efforts to promote equality.
  - X_8: Political expertise. 0–8 scale of factual political knowledge, with higher scores indicating more information and "sophistication."[13]

a.   What kind of variable is gender? _____

b.   Write out the regression equation for this model.

_____

_____

---

[13] Ibid., 164–66.

c. Provide a short verbal interpretation of the partial regression coefficient for income (X_3). Assume you are explaining to someone who is familiar with political science but not multiple regression.

_____

_____

_____

d. Give a substantive interpretation or explanation of the coefficient for gender (X_2).

_____

_____

_____

e. Consider only men (that is, assume $X_2 = 0$). If all of the other variables have scores of 0, what is the predicted value of the dependent variable?

f. Can you offer a substantive interpretation of this value? That is, explain its meaning to a politician.

_____

_____

_____

_____

g. Again consider just male respondents. What is the numerical effect of being African American if all other variables besides race have scores of 0? (Admittedly, this assumption doesn't make much sense—no one could be in the 0th income quartile, for example—but doing so makes it easier to interpret the individual coefficients.)

_____

h. Consider an African American female (that is, $X_1 = X_2 = 1$) with an expertise score of $X_8 = 2.87$. Assume all the other variables are 0. What is the predicted opposition scale score?

_____

i. The author of this study reports that the average score for economic individualism (X_6) is 13.70 and the mean for equal opportunity opposition (X_7) is 3.53.[14] Consider an African American female independent (that is, $X_4 = 3$) with an expertise score (X_8) of 2.57 and in the second quartile of income ($X_3 = 2$). Assume the score on feelings toward beneficiaries (X_5) = 50. If this person has average scores on individualism and equal opportunity opposition, what would be her predicted score on opposition to social welfare?

_____

_____

[14] Ibid., table A, 176.

j. Suppose this same individual switches to strong Democrat from independent but retains the same char-
    acteristics (measures) on all the other variables in the previous question. What is the effect of this change
    in party identification? _____ What is her predicted value on Y, social welfare policy
    opposition? _____

k. What does the observed F with 9 and 637 degrees of freedom tell you?

    _____

    _____

    _____

l. Given the N in the table, what is the appropriate sampling distribution to test the significance of individual
    coefficients?

    _____

m. The standard errors for the coefficients appear in table 14–7. What is the observed test statistic for gender?
    Is it statistically significant at the .05 level? At the .01 level? (Use a two-tailed test for both tests.)

    _____

n. What is the observed test statistic for political expertise (X_8)? Is it statistically significant at the .05 level? At
    the .01 level? (Use a one-tailed test.)

    _____

o. What does the R^2 tell you about the fit of the data to the model?

    _____

    _____

Exercise 14–8.   You and your best friend are working on a joint project about the role of religion in American
politics. In particular, you want to know if people of different religious faiths disagree with respect to their
evaluations of various political leaders and groups. You suggest using the 2002 American National Election
Study because it has feeling thermometers for many public officials, interest groups, and parties. These variables can be treated as numeric since the respondents can place themselves anywhere on a 100-degree (point)
scale. (For examples, look at the "anes2000" files on the Web site http://edge.sagepub.com/johnson8e.) But your
friend objects that the main independent variable is nominal and that respondents are simply assigned to the
categories "Protestant," "Catholic," "Jewish," "None," and "Other."[15] He's worried that you won't be able to take
advantage of regression analysis, which the instructor wants you to use. Do you have an answer for this person's
concern? What is it? How can you regress, say, feelings toward former President George W. Bush on religion?
Be specific to demonstrate your knowledge of the method.

    _____

    _____

_____

[15] The study has many codes for religion, but assume you want to use just those five.

_____

_____

_____

Exercise 14–9. Your boss has asked you to critique a paper, "The Causes of Crime in Urban America." The authors have data on about seventy-five cities. Among many other analyses, there is a regression of Y, violent crime rate (offenses per 100,000 population in 1992), on X_1, per capita income in central cities, and X_2, per capita expenditures for public safety. (These data can be found in the files "stateofcities.dat" or "stateofcities.por" on the Web site http://edge.sagepub.com/johnson8e.[16]) Luckily, some summary statistics for the variables have been supplied in an appendix to the report (table 14–8).

TABLE 14–8
Summary Statistics on Urban Crime

Variable	Valid Cases	Minimum	Maximum	Mean	Standard Deviation
Crime rate (Y_2)	69	141	3,859	1,573.00	88.158
Per capita income (X_1)	77	$9,258	$19,695	$13,679.56	$2,410.431
Per capita safety expenditures (X_2)	77	$101	$1,133	$280.43	$128.018

Source: Norman Glickman, Michael Lahr, and Elvin Wyly, "The State of the Nation's Cities: Database and Machine Readable Documentation," Version 2a (January 1998), Center for Urban Policy Research, Rutgers University.

a. The paper reports that the partial regression coefficient of crime on per capita income $(\widehat{b}_{YX_1})$ is –.0076. Does this number mean that economic well-being in a city is unrelated to crime? Explain.

_____

_____

_____

_____

_____

b. The standard error of this partial regression coefficient is .041. What is the observed t?

_____

_____

[16] The data are from Norman J. Glickman, Michael Lahr, and Elvin Wyly, "The State of the Nation's Cities: Database and Machine Readable Documentation," version 2a (January 1998), Rutgers University: Center for Urban Policy Research.

c. Assuming that there is a constant and two independent variables in the equation and $N = 66$ for this model, would you reject the null hypothesis that the population partial regression coefficient of crime rates on income is 0 based on a two-tailed test at the .05 level? Why or why not?

_____

_____

_____

_____

d. Now examine the second independent variable in the model, per capita city government spending on public safety (for example, police and fire protection). The partial regression coefficient of crime on this variable is 3.090. What does this result mean in substantive terms? More specifically, does it represent evidence of a cause-and-effect relationship? Why or why not?

_____

_____

_____

_____

_____

e. The standard error of the partial regression coefficient of Y on X_2 is .749. Knowing this, do you think the null hypothesis of no partial linear association between crime and public safety spending should be rejected? Why or why not?

_____

_____

_____

_____

_____

f. You notice that the report concludes that expenditures for police have a greater impact on crime than a city's standard of living. To make the point, the authors mention that the expenditure-standardized regression coefficient is twice the size of the one for per capita income, but, strangely, they do not report the actual values. Can you calculate them? And, more importantly, is there any reason at all to make that inference based on these data? (*Hint:* Look at table 14–7 for the statistics you need. Note, however, that the table contains some extra information. You need to select the right statistics. Refer to the section on standardization in chapter 13 of the textbook.)

_____

_____

_____

_____

_____

Exercise 14–10. Martin Gilens and Craig Hertzman raise a crucial point for judging the condition of American democracy. They studied news coverage of the 1996 Telecommunications Act, which, among other things, loosened restrictions on the number of television stations a media corporation could own. Some companies own both newspapers and local TV stations, whereas others do not. The passage of the law, the authors assert, meant that "on average the loosening of ownership caps in the 1996 Telecom Bill benefited media companies that already owned many television stations, and did not benefit (and may have hurt) companies that did not own TV stations."[17]

Some of their findings "strongly indicate a relationship between the financial interests of newspaper owners and the content of their papers' news coverage." This is not a matter of editorial content. Instead, the study's authors believe that what appears and *does not* appear in a paper's news sections may reflect the economic self-interests of the publisher and not inherent newsworthiness or the needs of the public. But they are aware that the connection between financial interest and news content may be "spurious, due to other characteristics of the newspapers."[18]

To check this possibility they conducted a multivariate analysis, a portion of which appears in table 14–9. The unit of analysis (twenty-seven in all) is "newspaper." The dependent variable is the proportion of a paper's coverage of the act that was "negative" (that is, discussed the possible adverse consequences of the Telecommunications Act). One of the independent variables was total weekly circulation, which provides an indicator of a paper's revenues, which in turn determine the size of its "news hole," or space for news content. ("Papers with higher circulations and larger news holes might be expected to publish more information about the telecommunications legislation and might mention a higher percentage of negative consequences as a result."[19]) The researchers also looked at presidential candidate endorsements as a proxy measure of the paper's political leanings and the percentage of revenue from broadcast television "to test the possibility that reporting on [the bill] was influenced less by the number of stations owned than by the parent company's economic dependence on TV revenue."[20] The investigators broke the main explanatory factor—ownership of television stations—into two dummy variables:

Substantial = 1 if company has nine or more TV stations in 1995
            0 if company owned none

Limited = 1 if company owned two to five TV stations in 1995
        0 if company owned none[21]

TABLE 14–9

Corporate Ownership and News Bias

	Estimated Coefficient	Standard Error	*t* Statistic	Level of Significance (two-tailed)[a]
Substantial	−.39	.13		
Limited	−.23	.12		
Circulation	.04	.02		
Endorsement	.04	.05		
Percentage of revenue from TV	−.05	.35		
$R^2 = .35$; $N = 27$				

[a]The researchers used a one-tailed test.

---

[17] Martin Gilens and Craig Hertzman, "Corporate Ownership and News Bias: Newspaper Coverage of the 1996 Telecommunications Act," *Journal of Politics* 62 (May 2000): 372.

[18] Ibid.

[19] Ibid.

[20] Ibid.

[21] It is not clear why Gilens and Hertzman chose this particular way to measure ownership, but the interpretation of the results is straightforward if you keep in mind the definition of dummy variables. Gilens and Hertzman, "Corporate Ownership and News Bias," table 3, 382.

Assume that the researchers have a random sample of newspapers. The table gives you part of the results from their regression analysis plus space to write some of your answers.

a. Write a model or equation for the predicted value of the proportion of negative coverage. (They didn't report a constant, so just ignore that coefficient.)

_____

_____

_____

_____

_____

b. Interpret R^2.

_____

_____

_____

_____

_____

c. Interpret in statistical and substantive terms the coefficients for substantial and limited ownership. (*Hint:* Refer to the discussion of dummy variables in chapter 13 of the textbook. Try to understand them using the logic employed in that section.)

_____

_____

_____

_____

_____

_____

d. What are the observed t values? Write them in table 14–9.

e. If you wanted to test each coefficient for significance using a two-tailed test, what would be the critical t at the .05 level? (It's hard to tell from the authors' explanation, so assume twenty-two degrees of freedom.)

_____

Which of the coefficients is significant at that level? Indicate with a "Yes." Better still, give the level of significance.

_____

_____

Exercise 14–11. Suppose that for a comparative government class you want to study the effect of globalization on citizens' political beliefs and behavior. You decide to concentrate on Britain's membership in the European Union (EU), a transnational organization of European states that some Britons fear will infringe on British sovereignty. In particular, you want to know if positions on this issue affected party and candidate choices in the 2001 British general election. Table 14–10 _summarizes_ the results of a cross-tabulation of responses to the question, "Overall, do you approve or disapprove of Britain's membership in the European Union?" and the party the respondents voted for in that election (Labour, Liberal Democrat, or Conservative). Your hypothesis is that those who support membership in the EU will vote Labour, whereas those against it will support the conservatives. (These numbers come from the British Election Study 2001 and can be found in the files "bes2001.dat" or "bes2001.por" on the Web site http://edge.sagepub.com/johnson8e.)

a. Try to replicate our findings in table 14–10. We eliminated all the minor parties—that is, Greens, SNP, Plaid Cymru, and "Other"—as well as "None." Your table won't match ours exactly unless you do the same.[22] Why?

TABLE 14–10

Results of Cross-Tabulation

Chi-square	df	Tau-b	Gamma	N
160.516	8	.190	.274	1,918

b. More importantly, interpret the results in the table. Supply both a statistical _and_ a substantive answer to the question, "Is there a relationship between opinions on the EU and the direction of the vote?"

_____

_____

_____

_____

_____

c. Party identification (partisanship) has been found to have a strong connection with voting: party loyalists usually back their parties in elections. So perhaps the relationship you saw in 14–11b (assuming that you think there is one) can be explained by the effects of party affiliation on those two variables. As the text indicates in chapter 13, one way to find out is to control for partisanship by creating subtables based on the categories of the control variable. In other words, the previous cross-tabulation, from which the chi-square, tau-b, and gamma were determined, was a 3 × 4 table. To hold party identification constant we generated three such 3 × 4 tables, one for each level of party identification. (_Reminder:_ For simplicity's sake, we are considering only the three major British parties.) Table 14–11 shows the results when we examined the attitude by vote relationship within the three categories of the control variable, party identification.

---

[22] We coded the vote variable this way: 1 = Labour, 2 = Liberal Democrat, and 3 = Conservative. We did so because we wanted the scores to run from least to most conservative.

TABLE 14–11

Results of Multivariate Analysis

Subtable	"Level" of Party Identification	Chi-Square	df	Tau-*b*	Gamma	*N*
1	Labour	16.992	8	−.04	−.11	919
2	Liberal Democrat	4.076	8	.03	.156	250
3	Conservative	47.347	8	.16	.41	566

Again, you might try replicating these findings by controlling for party identification (variable 01). In any event, try to interpret these results. Does the *party* variable explain or cancel the original relationship? (*Hint:* [1] Reread the section of chapter 13 on multivariate analysis of categorical variables. [2] Compare each of the statistics in this table with the corresponding ones in the previous attitude by vote table. [3] Try calculating a [weighted] average of tau-b or gamma or both and then compare it to the measure in the two-way table.)

_____

_____

_____

_____

_____

Exercise 14–12. Chapter 1 of the textbook described a study that showed the deleterious effects of negative campaigning on voter turnout.[23] This important finding did not go unchallenged, however. In the spirit of replication that we discussed in Chapter 2, political scientists Martin Wattenberg and Craig Brians published an article that "directly contradict[s] their findings."[24] They rested their case partly on the analysis of two surveys, the American National Election Studies for 1992 and 1996. The main independent variables were indicators of whether or not respondents remembered hearing or seeing negative and positive political advertisements and whether they made comments about these ads—that is, the variables were coded 1 if "Yes, comments were made" and 0 if "No." The dependent variable was a dichotomy: Did the respondent vote or not? The researchers hypothesized that if being aware of attack ads does adversely affect citizenship, there should be a negative correlation between commenting on attack ads and voting. If, by contrast, exposure to such ads had little effect on potential voters, the relationship would be nil.

Besides these variables, they also included many other independent factors that might affect the decision to vote. Table 14–12 presents a small portion of their results for the 1996 survey respondents.[25]

_____

[23] Stephen D. Ansolabehere, Shanto Iyengar, and Adam Simon, "Replicating Experiments Using Aggregate and Survey Data: The Case of Negative Advertising and Turnout," *American Political Science Review* 93 (December 1999): 901–10.

[24] Martin P. Wattenberg and Craig Leonard Brians, "Negative Campaign Advertising: Demobilizer or Mobilizer," *American Political Science Review* 93 (December 1999): 891.

[25] Ibid., table 3, 894. The Wattenberg and Brians model contains other control variables. We eliminated them to keep things simple.

TABLE 14–12

Logistic Regression of Turnout on Advertising Recall and Other Variables

Variable	Partial Coefficient	Standard Error
Negative ad comment: 1 = yes, 0 = no	−.2005	.1792
Positive ad comment: 1 = yes, 0 = no	.2652	.2806
Newspaper political news index[a]	.0337	.0113
Age in years	.0295	.0054
Campaign interest: 1 = somewhat, 0 = otherwise	.3824	.1672
Campaign interest: 1 = very much, 0 = otherwise	2.0460	.3260
Gender: 1 = female, 0 = male	.3195	.1533
Time from interview to election (in days)	−.0053	.0043
Independent leaner:[b] 1 = independents who lean toward a party, 0 = otherwise	.8183	.2647
Weak partisan:[b] 1 = weak partisan, 0 = all others	.7279	.2543
Strong partisan:[b] 1 = strong partisan, 0 = all others	1.7830	.2935
Race: 1 = white, 0 = nonwhite	.1962	.2057
Constant	−4.4223	.4223

N = 1,373. Percentage of respondents correctly predicted 81 percent, based on these variables plus others not in this table.

[a] Coded on scale from 0 to 28 with 28 being highest interest.

[b] Pure independent treated as reference category.

a. The coefficients in the table constitute the terms of a logistic regression model. Write the model as an expression for the predicted probability of voting.

b. Write the model as an expression for the estimated log odds (logit) of voting.

c. If someone had null (zero) values on all of the variables, what would be his predicted probability of voting? (By the way, why do we write *his* here?)

What is the substantive interpretation of this probability? Does it make any sense?

d. Now suppose a person is fifty years old but has null values on all the independent variables. Before doing any calculations, look at the coefficient for age. Do you think this estimated probability would be higher than the previous one? Why?

_____

_____

_____

_____

e. What is the predicted probability of voting for this fifty-year-old man? _____

In words, what is the effect of age on the likelihood of voting when everything else is the same?

_____

_____

_____

f. Consider this same person. What are the estimated *log* odds that he will vote? _____

What are the estimated *odds* that the individual will go to the polls on Election Day? _____

Write a commonsense interpretation of this latter estimate.

_____

_____

_____

g. Consider a sixty-year-old white female who is a strongly partisan Democrat, mentioned both negative and positive commercials, has a score of fourteen on the political news index, is very interested in the campaign, and was interviewed five days before the election. What is the predicted probability that this person will vote? What are the odds of her voting? (*Hint:* List this woman's values on each of the variables. [For instance, if she is "very interested," how would she be coded on that and the other interest variable?] Then substitute the values for these variables into the equation for the predicted probability.)

_____

_____

_____

_____

_____

h. Compare the person in 14–12g with an identical male. Who is more likely to vote? Why?

_____

_____

_____

_____

_____

_____

i.   Which of the coefficients in the table are significant?

_____

_____

_____

_____

_____

j.   In your view, are the authors correct in saying that exposure to negative political commercials does not depress turnout? (*Hint:* Think about the main independent variable. Then consider a "typical" person, as we did in some of the previous questions. Get the estimated probability or odds of voting for this individual both when he or she mentions negative ads [that is, when the score is 1] and when no negative commercials are mentioned. How much do the probabilities or odds change?)

_____

_____

_____

_____

_____

Exercise 14–13.   Multiple regression offers the opportunity to test whether the relationship between variables holds up in the presence of control variables. Consider, for example, the relationship between the number of craft breweries in a state and the percentage vote for Barack Obama in each state in 2012. Open the "States" data file available on the PSRM Web site in the statistical package chosen by your instructor and answer the questions below. Use a two-tailed test and a 95 percent confidence level when assessing statistical significance.

a.   Run an ordinary least squares regression using the *beer* variable as the independent variable and *votepercentobama2012* as the dependent variable. Attach your results. Interpret the relationship between the number of craft breweries in a state and the vote percentage for Obama. Make sure you interpret the coefficient and statistical significance.

_____

_____

b.   Why might this result be flawed? Is there substantive significance?

_____

_____

c. Run a second regression that adds another independent variable, *conservative*, that measures the percentage of conservative voters in each state. Attach your regression output. Interpret this regression, making sure to include a discussion of coefficients and statistical significance.

_____

_____

d. What happened to the relationship between beer and percentage vote for Obama when controlling for the percentage of conservatives in each state? Why do you think this happened?

_____

_____

_____

_____

_____

Exercise 14–14. Continuing from exercise 14–13, examine additional variables in the "States" file that might predict Obama's vote percentage in 2012. Select two more variables to add to the multiple regression you executed above with beer and conservative.

a. What do you expect to see when you add your additional two variables?

_____

_____

b. Run your new regression with beer, conservative, and two additional independent variables and vote percentage for Obama as the dependent variable. Interpret the results, making sure to include a discussion of each coefficient and statistical significance.

_____

_____

_____

_____

_____

_____

c. Did you find any unexpected results?

_____

_____

HELPFUL HINTS

Preparing and Organizing a Multivariate Analysis

Analyzing more than two variables at a time can be a daunting chore, even for experienced data analysts. The secret, we believe, is the same as for any academic undertaking: think before acting. In the case of multivariate analysis, careful planning is of utmost importance. Hence, we offer a few suggestions to help you organize your research:

■ As we discussed in previous chapters of the textbook, it is essential that you state a few working hypotheses. If you sit in front of a computer before organizing your thoughts, you will soon be drowned in printout. We guarantee it.

■ If you are given a data set, pick a likely dependent variable—something that might be important to understand or explain. Then ask yourself which of the other variables in the file might be related to it. If you are starting from scratch, you have more leeway. But in any case try to convert these ideas into substantive hypotheses. (Remember, a hypothesis is a tentative statement subject to verification. The result of the test is less important than starting with a meaningful proposition. Why? Because whether one accepts or rejects it, something of value has been learned. Testing trivial propositions [for example, poverty among children is correlated with poverty among families] doesn't advance our knowledge of anything.)

■ Similarly, think carefully about what would be appropriate indicators of general explanatory factors. Suppose, for instance, you believe high crime rates encourage people to leave cities for the suburbs or countryside. If you are trying to explain migration to the suburbs, one of your independent variables would be crime, which can be measured by, say, homicide rates or property lost to theft. Whatever the case, think of broad explanatory factors and empirical indicators of those factors.

■ Sometimes the choice of variables is straightforward. Frequently, however, you may need your imagination to construct indicators. Suppose you theorize that changes in population density explain something, but the data at your disposal contain only the actual populations and areas of cities for 1994 and 2004. You first need to compute a density for each year by dividing total population by area to obtain, say, persons per square mile. Then you could calculate another indicator, "percentage change in population density from 1994 to 2004."[a] Most software programs make these sorts of transformations easy.

■ Remember that the data are empirical indicators of underlying theoretical concepts. You can't expect them to be perfectly or even strongly related to the dependent variable or to one another. In general, if you find a model that explains 40 to 50 percent of the statistical variation in Y, you will be doing well.

■ We strongly urge you to analyze each variable individually, especially the dependent variable. Use the methods described in chapter 11 of the textbook.

■ If your analysis involves multiple regression, first obtain plots of all the variables against each other. Doing so will reveal important aspects of the relationships, such as curvilinearity, the existence of outlying points, and the lack of variation in one or both variables. All these aspects can and should be taken into consideration.

■ It is permissible, even advisable in some instances, to delete the outlying cases if you can do so on substantive grounds. Or you can sometimes transform variables. Have you noticed, for instance, that some authors we cite in this book analyze not income but the logarithm of income? Doing so can mitigate the effects of a few very large numbers on a statistical procedure. One of the unfortunate properties of regression as we have introduced it is that it can be very sensitive to extreme scores. Hence, you may find that a statistical result changes considerably after adjusting the data.[b] Just be sure to describe your methods fully in your report.

(Continued)

(Continued)

■ It helps to obtain a correlation matrix of your variables. This table will point to variables that are not related to much of anything and that might be dropped from the analysis. Equally important, correlation coefficients will help you decide whether an independent variable is related in the way your hypothesis predicts. If there should be a negative relationship, for instance, and the correlation is positive, your starting assumption may be wrong or you may have to look more carefully at the variable's definition.

■ A correlation and a plot can also flag another possible problem. Sometimes two independent variables are so highly correlated that they are practically equivalent to each other, and including both in a regression model just adds redundancy; no separate information gets included.

After all, if you regress height on weight measured in pounds and in kilograms, you just have two versions of one concept. Thus, if you spot high intercorrelations among the independent variables, ask if they are measuring the same thing or represent interesting substantive relationships.

Your final model may be much simpler than your initial expectations. That's probably a good thing because the goal of science is to find the simplest equation that has the highest predictive capacity. It is not important to include lots and lots of variables. One technique is to add or subtract one variable at a time and determine if it appreciably changes the model.[c] You may be able to eliminate quite a few variables this way, thereby reducing complexity.

---

[a] We recommend the log percent change, which is $\log^{10}$ (first number/second number) $\times$ 100, where $\log^{10}$ is the logarithm to the base 10.

[b] Trust us: far from "cooking the books," this maneuver is acceptable statistical practice in many instances.

[c] Lots of software programs have procedures for automating this process, but we don't recommend using them at this stage.

Exercise 14–15. The Web site http://edge.sagepub.com/johnson8e contains several other files of various types. Pick an issue or a problem in political science or politics and see if there are data on the Web site that might be appropriate for analyzing your chosen topic. You can use the procedures described at the beginning of this chapter to organize your thinking, even if the data are strictly nominal or ordinal.

Exercise 14–16. Dummy variables are an important type of variable in statistical analysis. Answer each of the following questions about dummy variables.

a. Define a dummy variable.

_____

_____

b. Why is a dummy variable typically assigned the values of 1 and 0?

_____

_____

c. How can a dummy variable be used to convert a categorical variable into a variable that can be used in higher-order statistical analyses? Provide an example of a categorical variable with a nominal level of measurement and explain how it could be transformed into at least one dummy variable.

_____

_____

_____

_____

d. Provide an example of how you might use a dummy variable in an interaction term in an analysis, such as ANOVA or regression. Imagine that you have two variables: income (a continuous variable) and gender (a dummy variable). Explain how you could interact the two variables for use in an analysis of political participation.

_____

_____

_____

_____

Exercise 14-17. Open the "Social Vote" data set available on the PSRM Web site in the statistical package chosen by your instructor. Find the _paille_ variable, which indicates whether the respondent encouraged anyone to vote for Barack Obama or Mitt Romney by posting on a social networking site, such as Facebook or Twitter, in the last thirty days. Select the cases where paille equals 1 or 0 and delete the other cases. Then, choose two variables that you think explain why individuals would use social media to ask others to vote for a candidate and include all three variables in a logistic regression model. Attach your results and interpret the results below. Make sure to interpret as much as you can about the coefficients and the model as a whole.

_____

_____

_____

_____

_____

_____

_____

_____